Bruno Paz

The New Laws of Power
Contemporary Strategies for Success

Copyright
Original Title: As Novas Leis de Poder
Copyright © 2024, published by Luiz Antonio dos Santos

This book explores modern strategies and psychological principles applied to personal and professional development, addressing aspects of self-awareness, emotional intelligence, and decision-making. It is intended for reflection and study and does not replace professional medical, psychological, or financial advice.

First Edition Production Team
Author: Bruno Paz
Editor: Luiz Antonio dos Santos
Graphic Design and Layout: Studios Booklas
Text Revision and Editing: Valéria Ramos
Translation: Ethan Parker

Publication and Identification
Strategic Power / By Bruno Paz
Booklas, 2024
Categories: Management / Applied Psychology
DDC: 658.4 - CDU: 159.9

Copyright Notice
All Rights Reserved to:
Booklas Publishing / Luiz Antonio dos Santos

This book may not be reproduced, distributed, or transmitted in whole or in part by any means, electronic or printed, without the express permission of the copyright holder.

José Delalíbera Street, 962
86.183-550 – Cambé – PR
Email: suporte@booklas.com
Website: www.booklas.com

Summary

Prologue 6
Law 1 Master Emotions 8
Law 2 Cultivate Intuition 12
Law 3 Conceal Your Intentions 16
Law 4 Speak Less 20
Law 5 Build Reputation 24
Law 6 Draw Attention 28
Law 7 Inspire Trust 32
Law 8 Master Narratives 36
Law 9 Plan Victories 40
Law 10 Avoid Conflicts 44
Law 11 Manage Dependency 48
Law 12 Offer Generosity 52
Law 13 Disarm Opposition 56
Law 14 Build Networks 60
Law 15 Master Information 64
Lei 16 Crie Urgência 68
Law 17 Master the Art of Negotiation 72
Law 18 Lead Change 77
Law 19 Build Alliances 81
Law 20 Manage Time 85
Law 21 Delegate Tasks 89
Law 22 Cultivate Creativity 93
Law 23 Master Technology 97
Law 24 Invest in Learning 101

Law 25 Promote Diversity 105
Law 26 Practice Resilience 110
Law 27 Communicate Effectively 114
Law 28 Use Language Effectively 119
Law 29 Captivate Audiences 123
Law 30 Present Ideas 127
Law 31 Manage Expectations 131
Law 32 Build Consensus 135
Law 33 Lead Teams 139
Law 34 Manage Conflicts 143
Law 35 Promote Collaboration 148
Law 36 Celebrate Achievements 152
Law 37 Provide Feedback 156
Law 38 Inspire Action 160
Law 39 Build a Legacy 164
Law 40 Take Risks 168
Law 41 Embrace Uncertainty 172
Law 42 Cultivate Self-Awareness 176
Law 43 Define Purpose 180
Law 44 Seek Mentorship 184
Law 45 Share Knowledge 189
Law 46 Practice Gratitude 193
Law 47 Promote Well-Being 197
Law 48 Build Balance 201
Law 49 Create Impact 205
Law 50 Reinvent Yourself 209
Law 51 Live with Purpose 213

Law 52 Transcend Limits 217
Epilogue 221

Prologue

Every line ahead has been written with a precise purpose: to transform what you believe you know about success and strategy. The text you hold in your hands is not just another collection of ideas but a carefully crafted tool designed to alter your perspective on control, influence, and self-mastery. Here, science and practice converge to provide an unprecedented view of how to navigate the challenges of the modern world.

You are about to enter a universe where emotional intelligence is as powerful as logic, and where mastering emotions and masking intentions can determine the outcome of any situation. This book distills principles grounded in data and evidence, refined by psychological and behavioral insights, into a narrative that goes beyond abstract theories. Every concept presented is designed to be applicable, tangible, and transformative.

Consider for a moment the magnitude of the choices you make daily—decisions that affect your career, relationships, and even your mental health. Now ask yourself: are you in control of these decisions, or are you driven by impulses and external circumstances? What you will find here is a roadmap of strategic power, a guide that dissects how leaders, innovators, and visionaries shape their realities.

This is not a manual for those seeking easy shortcuts. On the contrary, it demands that you face uncomfortable truths about what it truly means to master your emotions, cultivate intuition, and manage dependencies. The result, however, is freedom—the ability to navigate chaos with clarity, purpose, and precision.

Throughout these pages, you will discover the impact of narratives on the human mind, the quiet strength of strategic generosity, and the power of calculated communication. Each chapter functions as a piece of a larger puzzle, where the whole reveals a potential you may not even realize you possess. Science is on your side—from studies on emotional resilience to analyses of the importance of interpersonal relationships in building robust support networks.

This book is more than an invitation; it is a challenge. It confronts you to reevaluate not only your strategies but also your beliefs about what it means to live strategically. And as you explore its ideas, you may find that true power lies not just in achieving goals but in understanding the system behind every victory and defeat.

If you have made it this far, it is not by chance. This book was made for those who seek more, who refuse to be victims of circumstance and wish to take control of their journey. Now, all you need to do is turn the page.

Law 1
Master Emotions

Mastering your emotions is the foundation of a life of control, clarity, and fulfillment. When you take charge of what you feel, you transcend the limitations imposed by impulsive reactions and achieve a state of balance that turns challenges into opportunities.

Self-control is not a skill reserved for the few; it is an accessible capability that enhances your resilience, sharpens your mind, and strengthens your relationships. Every emotion, whether positive or negative, can be channeled as a powerful tool for your growth. You are not a prisoner of fear, anger, or anxiety—you are the master of your emotional narrative.

By understanding the triggers that activate your emotions and developing methods to manage them, you eliminate internal chaos and create space for rational decisions and effective strategies. This mastery goes beyond your personal life; it expands your empathy and increases your influence, allowing you to connect with and inspire others profoundly and meaningfully.

This is the initial step in a journey that transforms not only how you live but who you become. Mastering your emotions is the starting point for an existence where balance and fulfillment become more than aspirations—they become your reality.

Personal Advantages:

Self-control: Learning to control your emotions allows you to react calmly and thoughtfully in challenging situations, avoiding emotional outbursts that could harm your relationships and reputation.

Resilience: Developing emotional resilience helps you recover from setbacks and adversities more easily, turning challenges into growth opportunities.

Mental clarity: Controlling your emotions frees mental space to think more clearly and make more rational decisions based on logic rather than impulses.

Empathy: Understanding others' emotions allows you to connect with them on a deeper level, building trust and strengthening your relationships.

Influence: The ability to read and respond to others' emotions enhances your influence and persuasion, enabling you to communicate more effectively and inspire confidence.

Well-being: Mastering your emotions contributes to your mental and emotional well-being, reducing stress and anxiety and promoting inner peace.

Application Methods:

Self-awareness:

Identify emotional triggers: Pay attention to events, people, or situations that elicit strong emotional reactions. Keep a journal to record these triggers and your responses.

Recognize emotional patterns: Observe how you typically react in various situations. Do you get irritated easily? Do you withdraw under pressure? Identifying your patterns is the first step to changing them.

Practice self-monitoring: Pay attention to your thoughts, feelings, and physical sensations in the present moment. This increases your awareness and allows you to control your emotions before they control you.

Emotional Management:

Take deep breaths: When emotions run high, take a few deep breaths. Deep breathing calms the nervous system and reduces emotional intensity.

Reframe your thoughts: Challenge negative thoughts and replace them with more positive and realistic ones. For example, instead of thinking, "I'm a failure," think, "I made a mistake, but I can learn from it."

Step away: If overwhelmed by emotions, step away from the situation for a few minutes. Take a walk, listen to relaxing music, or do something you enjoy to calm down.

Express emotions healthily: Find healthy ways to express your emotions, such as talking to a friend, journaling, exercising, or engaging in creative activities.

Emotional Reading:

Observe body language: Pay attention to nonverbal cues like facial expressions, posture, gestures, and tone of voice. These reveal much about a person's emotions.

Listen attentively: Actively listen to what others are saying, focusing not only on their words but also on the tone and emotions behind them.

Ask questions: Pose open-ended questions to better understand others' perspectives and feelings.

Show empathy: Demonstrate that you care about and understand others' emotions.

Influence and Persuasion:

Build rapport: Create a genuine connection with others by showing interest in their lives and demonstrating empathy.

Communicate clearly: Express your ideas and emotions concisely, using language that is easy to understand.

Use body language effectively: Maintain an open, receptive posture, make eye contact, and use gestures that convey confidence and positivity.

Adapt communication: Tailor your communication style to the preferences of the person you are interacting with.

Step-by-Step Guide to Applying the Law "Master Emotions":

Begin with self-awareness: Reflect on your emotions, triggers, and patterns.

Practice self-monitoring: Be mindful of your thoughts, feelings, and physical sensations throughout the day.

Develop emotional management skills: Try techniques like deep breathing, thought reframing, and healthy emotional expression.

Enhance emotional reading skills: Observe body language, listen actively, and show empathy.

Apply your knowledge to interactions: Use your emotional intelligence to build stronger relationships, communicate effectively, and influence others positively.

Adjustments if Expected Results Do Not Occur:

Struggling to control emotions: Seek professional help from a therapist or counselor.

Difficulty reading others' emotions: Practice observing people in different situations and interpreting their nonverbal cues.

Unsatisfactory interaction outcomes: Review your strategies and try different approaches.

Examples:

In conflict situations: Instead of reacting impulsively with anger, take deep breaths, step away for a few minutes, and approach the conflict constructively once calmer.

In negotiations: Observe the other person's body language to identify weak points and adjust your negotiation strategy.

When leading a team: Show empathy and understanding to build trust and motivate colleagues.

Mastering emotions is a journey that requires practice and self-awareness. By developing emotional intelligence, you will be better equipped to face life's challenges, build stronger relationships, and achieve your goals. Remember, emotions are a natural part of the human experience but need not control you. By mastering them, you take control of your life and pave the way for success and personal fulfillment.

Law 2
Cultivate Intuition

Trusting your intuition is a decisive step in transforming how you make decisions and connect with the world. Your intuition is an internal compass that transcends immediate logic, guiding you along paths often invisible to the rational mind. Cultivating this ability opens the doors to a deeper understanding of yourself and others, allowing you to make swift, creative decisions aligned with your most genuine values.

Intuition is more than instinct. It is a powerful tool that combines your past experiences and subconscious into clear and effective insights. By enhancing your connection with this capacity, you uncover answers where there was once uncertainty, find innovative solutions to complex challenges, and perceive nuances in situations others might overlook.

This skill does not develop by chance; it grows through specific, conscious practices. Silencing mental noise, interpreting your body's signals, and trusting the wisdom that arises in silence are the pillars that strengthen your intuition. When you learn to listen to this inner voice, your decisions become not only quicker but also more assertive and authentic.

Cultivating your intuition means taking control when logic fails or time is limited. It leads to a state of clarity and self-confidence that transforms every aspect of your life—from the most routine decisions to the most impactful choices. Intuition is the bridge that connects you to your essence, amplifying your self-awareness, creativity, and well-being.

Personal Advantages:

Quick and effective decision-making: Intuition enables you to make fast and efficient decisions in complex situations, even when there isn't enough time or information for complete rational analysis.

Creativity and innovation: Intuition unlocks new ideas and innovative solutions, allowing you to think outside the box and find original answers to challenging problems.

Self-awareness: Connecting with your intuition deepens your understanding of your values, beliefs, and desires, contributing to self-knowledge and confidence.

Risk management: Intuition can alert you to potential dangers and risks, helping you avoid pitfalls and make safer decisions.

Interpersonal connection: Intuition allows you to connect with others on a deeper level, understanding their emotions, motivations, and intentions.

Well-being: Trusting your intuition increases your sense of control and self-confidence, reducing stress and promoting mental and emotional well-being.

Application Methods:

Quiet the Mind:

Meditation: Regular meditation calms the mind, reduces mental noise, and enhances receptivity to intuitive insights.

Mindfulness: Cultivate present-moment awareness by observing your thoughts and sensations without judgment. This deepens your connection to your intuition.

Silence: Dedicate time to silence and solitude, disconnecting from external distractions to allow your mind to settle.

Connect with Your Body:

Notice physical sensations: Your body sends subtle signals about situations and people. Learn to interpret these sensations, such as a tight stomach or a sense of lightness.

Gut feelings: Trust your instincts and "gut feelings" about situations and people. This type of intuition is quick and instinctive, rooted in past experiences and subconscious patterns.

Body language: Observe both others' body language and your own—it can reveal key information about emotions and intentions.

Stimulate Creativity:

Brainstorming: Use brainstorming techniques to generate new ideas and solutions, letting your mind explore possibilities without restrictions.

Visual thinking: Use mind maps, diagrams, and other visual tools to stimulate creativity and connect ideas intuitively.

Dreams: Pay attention to your dreams, which may carry messages and insights from your subconscious. Keep a dream journal to record and analyze them.

Trust Your Intuition:

Test your intuition: Start by trusting your intuition in small, everyday decisions. Observe the outcomes and adjust your actions as needed.

Follow your instincts: When you feel a strong sense about something, don't ignore it. Explore that feeling and see where it leads.

Embrace uncertainty: Your intuition won't always be correct. Be open to learning from mistakes and adjusting your decisions accordingly.

Step-by-Step Guide to Applying the Law "Cultivate Intuition":

Create an environment conducive to intuition: Dedicate time to quietude, meditation, and connecting with your body.

Pay attention to signals: Notice your physical sensations, dreams, and the cues in your surroundings.

Stimulate creativity: Explore different ways of thinking and generating ideas, such as brainstorming and visual thinking.

Trust your intuition: Start with small decisions and gradually build confidence in your instincts.

Reflect on your experiences: Analyze your decisions and their outcomes, learning from your successes and mistakes.

Adjustments if Expected Results Do Not Occur:

Difficulty quieting your mind: Experiment with different meditation and relaxation techniques until you find one that works for you.

Challenges connecting with physical sensations: Practice body awareness exercises such as yoga or tai chi.

Insecurity in trusting intuition: Begin with minor decisions and gradually increase your reliance on your instincts.

Examples:

In a business meeting: Pay attention to participants' body language to catch communication nuances and identify the true intentions behind their words.

Choosing a new job: Beyond analyzing rational aspects like salary and benefits, trust your intuition to assess if the company and culture align with your values and goals.

Making an important decision: Take time to reflect in silence, connect with your intuition, and listen to your inner voice.

In an increasingly complex and uncertain world, intuition is a powerful tool for navigating life's nuances and making more effective decisions. Cultivating intuition requires practice and persistence, but the benefits are immense. By trusting your intuition, you unlock new possibilities, creativity, and self-awareness. Remember, intuition is a skill that can be developed and refined over time. Invest in your intuitive development and reap the rewards of a more conscious, authentic, and fulfilling life.

Law 3
Conceal Your Intentions

Keeping your intentions hidden is more than a strategic choice—it's an essential asset for those who aim to operate effectively in competitive and unpredictable environments. By obscuring your goals, you create a veil of mystery that disarms adversaries, shields your plans from external interference, and enhances your capacity to act.

Mastering this skill grants invaluable freedom: the ability to act unnoticed and change course without drawing attention. While others focus on deciphering your intentions, you move quietly forward, turning discretion into power. Each subtle move, each false clue, enhances your ability to influence and negotiate with surgical precision.

Concealing intentions requires self-control, discernment, and a profound understanding of human behavior. Knowing when to speak, what to withhold, and how to divert attention demands more than tactics—it requires emotional intelligence. Those who master this art navigate complex situations with the skill of a strategist, maintaining a confident posture while executing actions that few notice until it's too late.

In the dynamic world of human and professional relationships, transparency is only a virtue when strategically appropriate. Knowing what to reveal and what to conceal isn't about manipulation but protection and strategy. This skill not only amplifies your chances of success but also builds authority and respect among those around you.

The true strength of concealing intentions lies in the freedom it provides. Used wisely, it allows you to achieve great feats without fanfare, preserving your energy and focus for what truly matters. By mastering this art, you control not only the unfolding of situations around you but also become the author of the very circumstances that shape your life.

Personal Advantages:

Element of surprise: Keeping your plans secret enables you to surprise opponents, disarming them and creating a strategic advantage.

Protection from sabotage: By hiding your intentions, you prevent adversaries from interfering with your plans or creating obstacles to block your objectives.

Freedom of action: Concealing your intentions gives you more freedom to maneuver and change strategies without raising suspicion.

Increased influence: Unpredictability enhances your power and influence as people struggle to anticipate your moves or counter your actions.

Strategic negotiation: Hiding your true intentions during negotiations allows you to secure concessions and advantages that wouldn't be possible if your goals were known.

Building trust: Discretion and secrecy inspire confidence, as people feel safer dealing with someone who doesn't reveal their plans to just anyone.

Methods of Application:

1. Cultivate Discretion:

Be selective about whom you confide in: Share your plans only with those of utmost trust who have a vested interest in your success.

Avoid gossip and speculation: Don't engage in discussions about others' plans or fuel gossip about your own.

Maintain a low profile: Avoid unnecessary attention and keep your actions and intentions under control.

2. Use Distraction:

Create smoke screens: Send false signals and distract attention from your true objectives.

Focus on secondary goals: Promote secondary goals to divert attention from your main plans.

Use misinformation: Spread false or misleading information to confuse opponents and mask your real intentions.

3. Master the Art of Deception:

Adopt a persona: Create a public image that conceals your true intentions and motivations.

Control your emotions: Maintain a neutral expression and regulate your emotions to avoid revealing your true intentions.

Use body language to your advantage: Keep a relaxed and confident posture, avoiding gestures or expressions that might betray your plans.

4. Be Strategic:

Plan your moves carefully: Consider all angles and anticipate potential reactions from opponents.

Adapt your strategy: Be ready to change your plans as needed, always keeping your objectives in mind.

Seize opportunities: Stay alert to emerging opportunities and know how to leverage them, even if it means deviating from your original plans.

Step-by-Step Guide to Applying "Conceal Your Intentions":

Define your goals: Be clear about what you want to achieve.

Identify your opponents: Recognize those who might try to hinder your progress.

Develop a strategy: Create a detailed plan including tactics to mask your intentions and divert your opponents' attention.

Implement your strategy: Execute your plan discreetly and carefully, adapting as needed.

Monitor your results: Evaluate your progress and make necessary adjustments to ensure you stay on track.

Adjustments if the Expected Results Do Not Occur:

If your plans are discovered: Adapt your strategy and create new distractions to confuse your opponents.

If you encounter unexpected resistance: Reassess your plans and identify new ways to overcome obstacles.

If you fail to achieve your goals: Analyze your mistakes and learn from them to improve future strategies.

Examples:

In competition: Spread rumors about your weaknesses to mislead opponents into underestimating your abilities.

In negotiation: Feign disinterest in a particular item to secure a better deal on something you truly want.

When seeking a promotion: Keep your plans confidential and continue working diligently without revealing your ambitions.

The skill of concealing intentions is a subtle dance between strategy and perception. Those who master this art understand that silence, discretion, and unpredictability are as powerful as any direct action. By hiding your true motivations, you not only protect your plans but create layers of complexity that confound adversaries and enhance your advantage.

However, this practice requires balance. The mask should be used wisely—not to deceive completely, but to protect what is most valuable: your goals and your freedom to act. It's not about manipulation but anticipation; not about hiding but preparing the ground for your actions to thrive at the right moment.

Remember: true mastery lies not in deceiving others but in knowing when and how to reveal your truth. After all, those who can conceal their intentions control not just their actions but also the impact they leave on the world.

Law 4
Speak Less

The power of your words is directly related to their rarity and precision. Speaking less is not merely an exercise in restraint but a strategic art that amplifies the impact of every idea conveyed. By choosing your words carefully, you not only avoid misunderstandings but create a space where silence becomes as eloquent as speech.

Those who master the skill of speaking less stand out in a world saturated with noise. Their message, clear and objective, cuts through the excess of information and leaves a lasting impression. Carefully considered words become tools of influence and persuasion, while strategic silence projects authority and mystery.

More than a communication skill, speaking less is a practice that transforms how you connect with others and with yourself. By listening more, you expand your understanding, strengthen your relationships, and avoid mistakes that could compromise your credibility. This balance between what is said and what is held in reserve is what separates effective communicators from those lost in empty discourse.

Speaking less does not mean omitting or restricting your voice but refining your expression. Every word counts, every pause reinforces, and the impact of your messages becomes undeniable. This is the path for those who wish to communicate not just ideas but strength and purpose.

Personal Benefits

Increased credibility: Speaking less and with purpose conveys confidence and competence. People tend to respect those who think before speaking and who do not waste words.

Greater persuasive power: Conciseness makes your messages more memorable and impactful. By eliminating excess information, your ideas stand out and are absorbed more easily.

Improved communication: Listening more than speaking allows you to better understand others' perspectives, avoid misunderstandings, and build stronger relationships.

Error reduction: Speaking less reduces the chances of saying something careless or contradictory, protecting your reputation and credibility.

Enhanced focus: Conciseness promotes mental clarity and focus, enabling you to concentrate on the essentials and avoid distractions.

Projection of power: Strategic silence can be a powerful tool of influence. It creates an aura of mystery and authority, encouraging others to work harder to understand your thoughts and intentions.

Methods of Application

Practice Active Listening

Pay attention: Focus on what the other person is saying, make eye contact, and avoid distractions.

Show interest: Ask questions, nod, and use facial expressions to show you are engaged in the conversation.

Paraphrase: Restate what the other person said in your own words to ensure you understood correctly.

Be Concise in Your Communication

Think before speaking: Organize your thoughts before you speak and choose your words carefully.

Get to the point: Eliminate irrelevant information and focus on the main message you want to convey.

Use short, clear sentences: Avoid long, complex sentences that may confuse your audience.

Use Strategic Silence

Pauses: Take strategic pauses during your speech to give your listeners time to absorb the information and to create suspense.

Reflective silence: After a question or comment, pause before responding to show that you are carefully considering your answer.

Silence as a response: In some situations, silence can be the most powerful response. It can express disapproval, disagreement, or simply make the other person feel uncomfortable and reveal more information.

Master the Art of Brevity

Emails: Write short, objective emails that go straight to the point.

Meetings: Prepare for meetings in advance and focus on discussing the most important topics.

Presentations: Create concise and impactful presentations, using visual aids to complement your speech.

Step-by-Step Guide to Applying the "Speak Less" Rule

Cultivate active listening: Practice mindfulness, show interest, and paraphrase what others say.

Be concise: Think before you speak, get straight to the point, and use short, clear sentences.

Use strategic silence: Pause, demonstrate reflection, and use silence as a response when appropriate.

Master brevity: Write concise emails, prepare for meetings, and create impactful presentations.

Adjustments If Desired Results Do Not Occur

Difficulty focusing on listening: Practice mindfulness exercises and meditation to improve concentration.

Tendency to talk too much: Record your conversations and analyze your speech patterns to identify areas for improvement.

Discomfort with silence: Practice silence in low-risk situations, such as during meditation or while observing nature.

Examples

In a negotiation: Make an offer and wait silently for the other party's response. Silence can pressure them into making concessions.

In a discussion: Instead of interrupting or raising your voice, listen attentively to what the other person has to say and respond calmly and concisely.

During a presentation: Use impactful images and graphics to communicate your ideas clearly and concisely, avoiding excessive text.

Conciseness is a reflection of clarity. By speaking less, you learn to listen more, think better, and act with greater purpose. This practice not only transforms how you communicate but also how you are perceived—as someone who inspires respect and confidence, someone whose words carry weight.

Remember: the true power of communication lies in the balance between sound and silence. Speaking less is not about saying little—it is about saying what is necessary, with intention and meaning.

Law 5
Build Reputation

Your reputation is your most valuable asset. It reflects your actions, values, and achievements in the eyes of others. A strong reputation not only opens doors but paves the way for success, creating a legacy that transcends time. It inspires trust, attracts opportunities, and amplifies your ability to influence.

Building a reputation requires more than competence; it demands consistency, authenticity, and a commitment to excellence. Every interaction, choice, and word contributes to shaping how others perceive you. Whether at work, in personal relationships, or in the public sphere, your reputation serves as your calling card, determining how you will be received and valued.

In today's interconnected world, where an image can be built or destroyed in seconds, cultivating a positive reputation is both a strategy and a necessity. It's not merely about seeking recognition but establishing a standard of integrity and excellence that inspires trust and respect.

Your reputation is not static; it grows or diminishes with each action. By mastering it, you transform your name into a symbol of credibility and influence, ensuring not only your place in the present but also your relevance in the future.

Personal Benefits

Trust and credibility: A solid reputation inspires confidence, opening the way for new opportunities and partnerships.

Influence and persuasion: With a good reputation, your words carry more weight, and your ideas are taken more seriously.

Attraction of opportunities: A positive reputation draws business opportunities, promotions, and collaborations.

Protection against attacks: A strong reputation acts as a shield against criticism and attacks, making you more resilient to damage.

Ease of access: People with good reputations find it easier to access resources, information, and influential individuals.

Enduring legacy: A positive reputation can leave a lasting legacy, inspiring and influencing others for generations.

Methods of Application

Cultivate Excellence

Master your skills: Dedicate yourself to improving your expertise and knowledge in your field.

Deliver high-quality work: Strive to produce excellent results in everything you do.

Pursue continuous improvement: Always seek new ways to learn and grow, staying current and relevant in your area.

Build Strong Relationships

Be reliable and ethical: Keep your promises, act with honesty, and uphold integrity in all situations.

Cultivate empathy: Show genuine interest in others, listen attentively, and seek to understand their perspectives.

Help others: Offer support without expecting anything in return, building a loyal and strong network.

Manage Your Public Image

Be authentic: Stay true to yourself and your values, projecting a consistent and genuine image.

Communicate clearly: Present your ideas concisely and persuasively, adapting to your audience and context.

Build your online presence: Use social media and other platforms to share your work, ideas, and values, creating a strong and positive personal brand.

Protect Your Reputation

Monitor your online reputation: Keep track of what people are saying about you online and respond to criticism constructively.

Defend your reputation: Address unfair or false attacks by correcting misinformation and safeguarding your image.

Learn from your mistakes: Everyone makes mistakes. Take responsibility, learn from them, and implement measures to avoid repeating them.

Step-by-Step Guide to Applying the "Build Reputation" Rule

Define your personal brand: Identify your values, skills, and goals, and how you want to be perceived by others.

Invest in your development: Seek opportunities to learn and grow, enhancing your skills and knowledge.

Build relationships: Connect with people in your field, fostering relationships built on trust and mutual respect.

Manage your online presence: Create a professional profile and share relevant content that showcases your expertise and values.

Monitor and protect your reputation: Track what people say about you and take steps to defend your image against attacks and criticism.

Adjustments If Desired Results Do Not Occur

Difficulty building relationships: Participate in events and activities that allow you to meet new people and network.

Negative online reputation: Take steps to correct misinformation, respond to criticism, and build a more positive online presence.

Mistakes that harm your reputation: Take responsibility for your actions, apologize, and implement measures to repair the damage.

Examples

A professional aiming to be recognized as an expert: Publishes articles in specialized journals, speaks at events, and shares knowledge on online platforms.

An entrepreneur seeking investors: Builds a reputation for innovation and success through their products, services, and success stories.

A public figure maintaining a positive image: Manages their social media presence, responds to comments and criticism, and participates in social initiatives.

Your reputation is a legacy in constant development. More than the words others use to describe you, it reflects the impact you leave on the world. Every choice is an opportunity to solidify this foundation or repair it when necessary.

Your reputation is your greatest ally. Nurture it with care, defend it with courage, and use it as a beacon to guide your actions and inspire those around you.

Law 6
Draw Attention

Drawing attention is not a whim; it's a strategic necessity in a world where being seen is the first step to being valued. Those who master the art of standing out not only capture eyes but also gain the power to shape perceptions, influence decisions, and unlock previously unreachable opportunities.

Visibility is influence. When you intentionally attract attention, you transform your work, talent, or ideas into points of reference, distinguishing yourself from the crowd. It's not just about being noticed but being remembered—creating a personal brand so impactful that it inspires trust, respect, and lasting recognition.

The ability to capture others' attention requires more than effort; it demands strategy, creativity, and authenticity. It's the combination of what you communicate, how you communicate, and to whom you communicate. From a confident presence to original content, every detail contributes to building a powerful image that not only attracts attention but sustains it.

Being seen is the start of any success journey. And those who master the attention of others don't just walk the stage of life—they command it, leaving a legacy that transcends the moment they are observed.

Personal Benefits:

Visibility and recognition: Drawing attention increases your visibility and recognition for your work, talent, or ideas.

Opportunities: Being noticed opens doors to new opportunities, whether professional, social, or personal.

Influence and persuasion: When you have people's attention, your messages carry more impact, making you more persuasive.

Personal branding: Drawing attention helps build a strong, memorable personal brand, setting you apart from the competition.

Boost in self-confidence: Being recognized and valued by others enhances your self-confidence and self-esteem.

Personal and professional growth: Visibility and recognition drive personal and professional growth, paving the way for success.

Application Methods:

Master the art of presentation:

Appearance: Dress appropriately for the context and the image you want to convey.

Body language: Use confident and expressive body language, make eye contact, gesture, and maintain an upright posture.

Verbal communication: Speak clearly, enthusiastically, and convincingly, using engaging and persuasive language.

Create relevant and original content:

Know your audience: Understand your target audience and create content that aligns with their interests and needs.

Provide value: Share useful information, interesting insights, and solutions to real problems.

Be original: Stand out from the competition by creating original, creative, and memorable content.

Use social media strategically:

Choose the right platforms: Identify the social media platforms most relevant to your audience and focus your efforts there.

Build a strong presence: Post content regularly, engage with your followers, and participate in relevant conversations.

Promote your work: Use social media to showcase your work, ideas, and projects.

Leverage personal marketing:

Networking: Attend events and conferences, connect with influential people, and build strategic relationships.

Public relations: Promote your work to the press, seeking opportunities to be interviewed, quoted, or invited to events.

Content marketing: Create and distribute relevant content to capture your audience's attention and establish your authority in your field.

Step-by-Step Guide to Applying the Law "Draw Attention":

Define your objectives: Determine what you aim to achieve by drawing attention (e.g., recognition, opportunities, sales).

Identify your audience: Understand the profile of your target audience and their interests.

Create a strategy: Plan how you will draw attention (e.g., original content, social media presence, events).

Implement your strategy: Execute your plan by creating and promoting relevant content and attending strategic events.

Monitor your results: Assess the impact of your actions and adjust as needed to optimize your outcomes.

Adjustments if the Expected Results Do Not Occur:

If your content is not reaching the desired audience: Review your dissemination strategy, experiment with different platforms and content formats.

If you are not connecting with your audience: Analyze their interests and needs, adapting your message and language accordingly.

If you're not receiving the expected feedback: Request feedback from trusted individuals and be open to constructive criticism.

Examples:

An artist seeking to promote their work: Organizes an exhibition in an unconventional location, creates a striking artistic performance, or uses social media to share their creative process.

An entrepreneur launching a new product: Develops a viral marketing campaign, offers an exclusive discount for early buyers, or sends free samples to digital influencers.

A professional looking for a new job opportunity: Updates their resume with relevant information, attends networking events, and proactively applies for positions.

The attention you earn reflects the value you offer to the world. It is the starting point for influencing, inspiring, and building a remarkable trajectory. However, being noticed is not enough; true impact comes from how you use that visibility to create genuine connections and turn opportunities into achievements.

Drawing attention is more than shining—it's using your light to illuminate the path you wish to follow, creating an impact that resonates far beyond the present moment.

Law 7
Inspire Trust

Trust is the foundation that sustains all meaningful and successful relationships. It is not just a desirable attribute but an essential requirement for fostering genuine connections, promoting collaboration, and cultivating a life of harmony and mutual respect. Inspiring trust does not happen by chance; it is a skill developed through authenticity, integrity, and consistent actions.

Being trustworthy is more than keeping promises—it's being a pillar of stability in uncertainty, an example of alignment between words and actions. Those who inspire trust are listened to more attentively, followed with greater conviction, and respected for their presence and values. This influence goes beyond words; it is reflected in how you treat others and how they feel around you.

Trust is built intentionally, brick by brick, through authentic gestures and honest interactions. When you act with empathy, respect differences, and remain present for those who rely on you, your reputation becomes a fortress, protected by your integrity and reinforced by your actions.

Cultivating trust invites reciprocity: by inspiring it in others, you also strengthen yourself, fostering relationships that transcend barriers and encourage mutual growth. It is a conscious choice that transforms not only who you are but what you represent to the world.

Personal Benefits:

Strengthened relationships: Trust is the foundation of any healthy relationship. Inspiring trust deepens bonds and creates more authentic and meaningful connections.

Improved communication: Trust enables open and honest communication, allowing you to express yourself freely and be understood more clearly.

Increased influence: Trustworthy individuals have greater influence, as their opinions and advice are taken seriously.

Enhanced collaboration: Trust promotes teamwork and cooperation, fostering an environment conducive to creativity and productivity.

Reduced conflicts: Trust helps prevent and resolve conflicts constructively, as people are more willing to communicate openly and find mutually acceptable solutions.

Better mental health: Trust-based relationships improve emotional well-being, reducing stress and anxiety.

Application Methods:

Be authentic and transparent:

Share your values: Be open about your values and beliefs, showing alignment between your words and actions.

Admit your flaws: Don't hesitate to acknowledge your mistakes and vulnerabilities. Honesty and humility inspire trust.

Communicate openly: Maintain open and honest communication, sharing relevant information and addressing questions transparently.

Demonstrate competence and reliability:

Keep your promises: Follow through on what you say and be punctual with your commitments. Reliability is fundamental to inspiring trust.

Show expertise: Share your knowledge and skills, demonstrating competence in your field.

Seek feedback: Be open to feedback and use it to improve your performance and abilities.

Cultivate empathy and respect:

Listen actively: Pay genuine attention to others, showing interest and empathy.

Respect differences: Value diversity and respect others' opinions and perspectives, even when you disagree.

Act with integrity: Treat everyone with respect and dignity, acting ethically and fairly in all situations.

Build strong relationships:

Invest time in your relationships: Dedicate time and energy to cultivating connections with friends, family, or colleagues.

Be present: Show up for important moments in the lives of those you care about, demonstrating support and affection.

Be dependable: Be there for others when they need you, offering your help and support.

Step-by-Step Guide to Applying the Law "Inspire Trust":

Be authentic: Stay true to yourself and act transparently in your interactions.

Demonstrate competence: Develop your skills and knowledge, and honor your commitments.

Cultivate empathy: Listen attentively, respect differences, and act with integrity.

Build relationships: Invest time and energy into relationships, be present, and remain dependable.

Adjustments If the Desired Results Do Not Occur:

If you struggle to open up to others: Start by sharing small details about yourself and gradually increase the level of intimacy.

If you make a mistake that undermines trust: Take responsibility for your actions, apologize, and take steps to rebuild lost trust.

If you have difficulty maintaining long-term relationships: Reflect on your behavior patterns and seek professional help if necessary.

Examples:

A leader aiming to inspire trust in their team: Shares their vision, sets clear expectations, delegates responsibilities, and acknowledges the team's efforts.

A professional seeking to build relationships with clients: Demonstrates expertise in their field, offers personalized solutions, and maintains transparent and effective communication.

A friend striving to strengthen bonds of friendship: Stays present through good and bad times, offers unconditional support, and communicates openly and honestly.

Trust is not a gift but a reflection of your actions and character. By inspiring trust, you build bridges that connect not only people but also ideas, values, and shared goals. Every authentic gesture and fulfilled promise contributes to a legacy of respect and collaboration.

Trust is a two-way street. By cultivating it in others, you also fortify it within yourself, creating a solid foundation for relationships that withstand the test of time and challenges.

Law 8
Master Narratives

Narratives are the soul of human communication. They not only inform but captivate, evoke emotions, and transform. Mastering the art of storytelling is the skill that distinguishes an ordinary message from a memorable experience capable of inspiring, persuading, and leaving a lasting impact.

When you master narratives, you shape perceptions and evoke emotions profoundly. Your ideas come to life through engaging characters, meaningful conflicts, and inspiring resolutions. A well-told story transcends words; it creates emotional connections that resonate deeply with the audience, fostering empathy and understanding.

Moreover, powerful narratives are not just creative tools—they are strategic weapons. They define how you are perceived, help build your personal brand, and allow you to control the narrative in critical moments. Whether in a speech, a presentation, an advertising campaign, or a simple conversation, a well-crafted story has the power to shape opinions and influence decisions.

Mastering narratives is more than creating stories; it's understanding how the power of words can connect, inspire, and transform. Those who master this art also master the impact they wish to leave on the world.

Personal Benefits:

Effective communication: Narratives make communication more effective by capturing the audience's attention, facilitating understanding, and making messages more memorable.

Persuasion and influence: Well-constructed stories have the power to persuade and influence people, stirring emotions, changing opinions, and motivating actions.

Personal branding: Authentic and engaging narratives help build a strong and memorable personal brand, connecting you with your audience on a deeper level.

Crisis management: Mastering narratives allows you to control the narrative in crisis situations, protecting your reputation and minimizing damage.

Inspirational leadership: Leaders who master storytelling inspire and motivate their teams, creating a sense of purpose and belonging.

Human connection: Narratives create emotional connections between people, fostering empathy, understanding, and collaboration.

Methods of Application:

1. Build engaging narratives:

Structure: Use a classic narrative structure with a beginning, middle, and end, creating a dramatic arc that keeps the audience engaged.

Characters: Create memorable and relatable characters with whom the audience can connect.

Conflict: Present a conflict that generates tension and keeps the audience in suspense, anticipating resolution.

Emotion: Explore human emotions to create an emotional bond with the audience, eliciting empathy, compassion, or joy.

2. Adapt the narrative to the context:

Audience: Tailor your narrative to the audience you wish to reach, considering their interests, values, and level of knowledge.

Objective: Define the purpose of your narrative and build the story around it, whether to persuade, inform, entertain, or inspire.

Medium: Choose the appropriate medium for your narrative, such as a speech, presentation, article, video, or social media post.

3. Control the narrative:

Framing: Define the framing of your narrative, emphasizing the aspects you want to highlight while minimizing those that may harm your message.

Language: Use persuasive language with tools like metaphors, analogies, and storytelling to captivate the audience and reinforce your message.

Contrast: Create contrasts between "before" and "after," "right" and "wrong," "hero" and "villain" to reinforce your message and make it more memorable.

4. Master storytelling tools:

Authenticity: Share real and authentic stories that convey your values and personality.

Details: Include vivid and sensory details in your narratives to make them more engaging and memorable.

Emotional connection: Create an emotional connection with the audience by sharing your own experiences and feelings.

Step-by-Step Guide to Applying the "Master Narratives" Law:

Define your goal: Determine what you want to achieve with your narrative.

Identify your audience: Understand your target audience and their interests.

Build the narrative: Create an engaging story with memorable characters, conflict, and emotion.

Adapt the narrative to the context: Adjust the story to the audience, objective, and communication medium.

Control the narrative: Use framing, language, and contrast to reinforce your message.

Adjustments If Desired Results Are Not Achieved:

If your narrative isn't engaging the audience: Review the story's structure, characters, and conflict.

If your message isn't being understood: Simplify the language and use examples and analogies.

If your narrative isn't persuasive: Strengthen the emotional connection with the audience and use more effective storytelling techniques.

Examples:

A politician seeking to convince voters: Shares personal stories that demonstrate their connection with people and their values.

A company launching a new product: Creates an advertising campaign with a compelling narrative showcasing the product's benefits.

A teacher explaining a complex lesson: Uses a story to illustrate the concept, making it more accessible to students.

Narratives are not just communication tools—they are bridges connecting ideas and people, creating a space where logic meets emotion. Storytelling is the skill that transforms information into inspiration, making every message an opportunity for genuine connection.

By mastering narratives, you don't just communicate—you shape realities, inspire actions, and leave your mark. Every story you tell is an extension of who you are and the impact you aim to create.

Law 9
Plan Victories

No victory is the result of chance. Planning victories is more than a strategy—it is the foundation upon which great successes are built. When you turn dreams into clear objectives and outline a detailed path to achieve them, every step becomes a calculated move toward success.

Planning is not merely organizing. It's about visualizing, anticipating, and preparing for the challenges and opportunities that will arise along the way. It's the act of creating a roadmap that directs your energy toward what truly matters, eliminating distractions and transforming potential difficulties into manageable steps.

Those who master the art of planning not only achieve more—they do so with efficiency, confidence, and purpose. Effective planning not only enhances productivity but also strengthens self-confidence, showing you are in control of your journey. It reduces stress by transforming uncertainty into clarity and anxiety into focused action.

Planning victories means deciding, with determination, that your goals are more than dreams. It's committing them to paper, action, and reality. This skill is the hallmark of winners, those who do not wait for perfect circumstances but create them.

Personal Benefits:

Clarity and focus: Planning your victories provides clarity about your goals and the path to achieve them, keeping you focused and motivated.

Organization and productivity: Good planning helps organize your time, resources, and activities, boosting productivity and efficiency.

Anticipation of problems: Planning ahead enables you to identify potential obstacles and develop strategies to overcome them, minimizing risks and unpleasant surprises.

Resource management: Effective planning helps manage your resources efficiently, whether they are financial, material, or human.

Increased self-confidence: Planning and achieving your goals boost your self-confidence and belief in your ability to turn dreams into reality.

Stress reduction: Good planning reduces stress and anxiety, as it makes you feel more in control of your life and future.

Methods of Application:

1. Set clear and specific goals:

Establish SMART objectives: Use the SMART methodology to set goals that are Specific, Measurable, Achievable, Relevant, and Time-bound.

Break down complex goals into smaller steps: If your goal is too complex, divide it into manageable and smaller tasks.

Visualize your goals: Picture yourself achieving your goals and feel the positive emotions associated with that accomplishment.

2. Create a detailed action plan:

Define the necessary steps: Identify the steps needed to achieve your goals.

Set deadlines: Establish realistic deadlines for each step of your plan.

Allocate resources: Determine the resources required for each step, such as time, money, materials, and people.

3. Anticipate obstacles and develop contingency strategies:

Identify potential problems: Consider possible obstacles you may encounter along the way.

Create alternative plans: Develop contingency plans to address potential problems, ensuring you have options if things don't go as planned.

Be flexible: Be prepared to adapt your plan as needed, as circumstances may change and new challenges may arise.

4. Monitor your progress and make adjustments:

Track your performance: Monitor your progress against the goals and deadlines set.

Evaluate your results: Analyze your outcomes to identify what's working and what needs improvement.

Adjust your plan: Revise your action plan as necessary based on your progress and results.

Step-by-Step Guide to Applying the "Plan Victories" Law:

Define your goals: Set clear, specific, and measurable objectives.

Create an action plan: Define the steps, deadlines, and resources needed to achieve your goals.

Anticipate obstacles: Identify potential problems and create contingency plans.

Monitor your progress: Track your performance, evaluate your results, and adjust your plan as necessary.

Adjustments If Desired Results Are Not Achieved:

If you struggle to define goals: Seek inspiration from people you admire, read books on planning and goal-setting, or hire a coach to guide you.

If your plan isn't working: Review your action plan, identify weaknesses, and make the necessary changes.

If unexpected obstacles arise: Stay calm, assess the situation, and adapt your plan to overcome the challenges.

Examples:

A student aiming to pass a competitive exam: Creates a study schedule, selects study materials, and takes mock tests to track progress.

An athlete preparing for a competition: Develops a training plan, sets performance goals, and monitors nutrition and rest.

An entrepreneur launching a new business: Prepares a business plan, secures funding, and defines marketing and sales strategies.

Planning is more than anticipating the future—it's shaping it. Every calculated step and every goal achieved reinforces your ability to transform intentions into accomplishments. In planning lies the power not just to achieve victories but to build a solid and inspiring trajectory.

Planning is the map that takes you from desire to realization. Carefully drawn, it not only guides you but also empowers you to overcome obstacles and celebrate every victory achieved.

Law 10
Avoid Conflicts

Avoiding conflicts is not a sign of weakness but a demonstration of wisdom and self-control. In a world where tensions can easily escalate, the ability to sidestep confrontations is a powerful tool for preserving your energy, protecting your reputation, and maintaining harmonious relationships.

Peace often does not arise from the absence of problems but from the conscious choice to avoid unnecessary confrontations. Avoiding conflicts is a strategic act that allows you to focus on greater goals, keeping your attention on what truly matters. It fosters healthy environments where respect, cooperation, and productivity flourish.

This skill requires more than silence. It demands clear communication, genuine empathy, and a diplomatic approach. Those who master the art of avoiding conflicts not only resolve tensions before they become problems but also build a reputation for balance and discernment that inspires trust and admiration.

Avoiding conflicts is more than retreating; it is acting deliberately to create harmony and pave the way for solutions that benefit everyone involved. It means transforming challenges into opportunities for collaboration and understanding.

Personal Benefits:

Energy preservation: Avoiding unnecessary conflicts conserves your physical and emotional energy, enabling you to focus on more productive and positive activities.

Reputation protection: Conflicts can tarnish your reputation and negatively affect your image. Avoiding unnecessary confrontations helps maintain your credibility and influence.

Relationship building: Avoiding conflicts contributes to creating and maintaining healthy relationships based on respect and cooperation.

Improved communication: The pursuit of peaceful solutions encourages dialogue and constructive communication, allowing you to express your needs and understand others' perspectives.

Increased productivity: Conflict-free environments are more productive, as people can concentrate on their tasks without distractions and tensions.

Inner peace: Avoiding conflicts fosters inner peace and emotional well-being, creating a more harmonious and balanced environment.

Methods of Application:

Identify risk situations:

Analyze the context: Be aware of signs indicating a potential conflict, such as differing opinions, competition for resources, or unexpected changes.

Know your triggers: Identify situations or people likely to provoke negative emotional reactions in you.

Observe body language: Pay attention to the body language of those around you, noting signs of tension, irritation, or aggression.

Communicate diplomatically:

Choose your words carefully: Communicate clearly, respectfully, and assertively, avoiding aggressive or accusatory language.

Practice active listening: Pay attention to what others say, aiming to understand their perspectives and needs.

Show empathy: Put yourself in the other person's position and try to view the situation from their perspective.

Negotiate and seek mutually acceptable solutions:

Be open to concessions: Be willing to compromise on some points to reach an agreement that satisfies all parties.

Explore alternatives: Be creative in seeking solutions that meet everyone's interests.

Find common ground: Focus on areas of agreement and use them as a foundation for building a joint solution.

Overcome obstacles and maintain peace:

Avoid direct confrontation: If possible, avoid direct confrontation and resolve differences more discreetly and diplomatically.

Stay calm: Take deep breaths, control your emotions, and avoid reacting impulsively in tense situations.

Step away if necessary: If the situation becomes too intense, step away to calm down and reflect on the best course of action.

Step-by-Step Guide to Apply the "Avoid Conflicts" Law:

Identify risk situations: Stay alert to signs of potential conflicts.

Communicate diplomatically: Speak with clarity, respect, and empathy.

Negotiate and seek solutions: Be open to compromises and explore alternatives.

Overcome obstacles: Avoid direct confrontations, remain calm, and step away if needed.

Adjustments if the Expected Outcome Does Not Occur:

If conflict is unavoidable: Prepare to defend your interests assertively but without aggression.

If you feel intimidated or threatened: Seek support from trusted individuals or relevant authorities.

If conflict escalates into violence: Prioritize your safety and leave the situation as quickly as possible.

Examples:

In a discussion with a colleague: Instead of retaliating with criticism, listen carefully and try to find common ground.

In a business negotiation: Be willing to compromise on some points to close a deal advantageous to both parties.

In a family conflict: Seek dialogue and mediation to resolve differences peacefully and constructively.

Avoiding conflicts is about preserving peace amidst chaos. By choosing diplomacy over confrontation, you strengthen relationships, protect your energy, and create an environment where cooperation can thrive.

Avoiding conflict does not mean avoiding problems but choosing a path that fosters balance and understanding. True strength lies in maintaining peace without sacrificing your values.

Law 11
Manage Dependency

Independence and dependency management are fundamental pillars for exercising power and achieving personal benefits in today's world. The ability to act autonomously, without being subject to external pressures, expands freedom of choice and strengthens resilience in the face of challenges. Conversely, strategic control over dependencies helps balance relationships, increase influence, and reduce vulnerabilities.

Self-sufficient individuals develop greater confidence and have more flexibility to explore opportunities. Diversifying resources, building support networks, and acquiring new skills are practices that promote solid and effective independence. At the same time, analyzing dependency dynamics—understanding who depends on you and who you depend on—helps identify power and control points in interactions.

Strategically managing dependencies enhances personal influence and impact. Practices such as intentional assistance, creating scarcity, and controlling information help consolidate advantageous positions, while maintaining viable alternatives and firm negotiations protects against manipulation.

Applying these strategies fosters greater autonomy and strengthens balanced and productive relationships. The science behind these practices offers clear paths to developing power, freedom, and resilience practically and effectively.

Personal Benefits:

Autonomy and freedom: Managing your own dependency increases autonomy and freedom, enabling decisions based on your interests and values, free from external pressures.

Negotiation power: Being less dependent on others strengthens your position in negotiations, allowing you to secure better outcomes and defend your interests more effectively.

Resilience to change: Independence makes you more resilient to change and uncertainty, as you have more resources and options to handle unexpected situations.

Self-confidence: Managing dependency boosts self-confidence by giving you a greater sense of control over your life and destiny.

Reduced vulnerabilities: Minimizing dependency on external factors decreases vulnerabilities and the risk of manipulation or exploitation.

Opportunities: Independence opens doors to new opportunities, as you have more freedom to pursue goals and explore new paths.

Methods of Application:

Cultivate independence:

Develop your skills: Invest in personal and professional growth by acquiring new skills and knowledge that increase self-sufficiency.

Diversify your resources: Avoid relying on a single source of income, information, or support. Diversify to reduce dependency on specific factors.

Build a network: Foster relationships with people who can provide support and assistance across different areas of life.

Analyze dependency relationships:

Identify who depends on you: Be aware of people who depend on you and how this affects your negotiating power and relationships.

Identify who you depend on: Recognize your own dependencies and how they may limit autonomy and freedom.

Evaluate power balance: Analyze the power dynamics in your interactions, identifying who holds greater influence and control.

Manage others' dependency:

Offer strategic help: Assist others strategically, creating a sense of obligation and reciprocity.

Create scarcity: Generate a perception of scarcity regarding your resources or skills to enhance your value and influence.

Control information: Manage the flow of information to maintain an advantage over those dependent on you.

Avoid being controlled by dependency:

Keep your options open: Avoid limiting yourself to a single option or path. Maintain flexibility and freedom of choice.

Negotiate firmly: Defend your interests confidently and resist pressures or blackmail.

Seek alternatives: If trapped in an unfavorable dependency, explore alternatives and create a plan to break free.

Step-by-Step Guide to Applying the "Manage Dependency" Law:

Cultivate independence: Develop skills, diversify resources, and build a support network.

Analyze dependency relationships: Identify who depends on you and whom you depend on.

Manage others' dependency: Offer strategic help, create scarcity, and control information.

Avoid being controlled: Keep options open, negotiate firmly, and seek alternatives.

Adjustments if the Expected Outcome Does Not Occur:

If becoming more independent is challenging: Identify obstacles hindering independence and create a plan to overcome them.

If you are being manipulated: Recognize signs of manipulation and take steps to protect yourself.

If unable to escape an unfavorable dependency: Seek professional help to overcome challenges and build a path to freedom.

Examples:

An employee seeking more negotiating power with their boss: Acquires new skills and knowledge to become more valuable to the company.

A supplier seeking greater control over clients: Creates an exclusive product or service and limits its availability.

An individual seeking freedom from an abusive relationship: Develops a plan for financial independence and seeks support from friends and family.

Managing dependency is essential for navigating the complex power dynamics of today's world. Cultivating independence increases autonomy, freedom, and negotiating power. At the same time, understanding and managing others' dependency enables you to influence people and achieve your goals more effectively.

Remember, dependency is a powerful tool. Use it wisely to build a freer, more authentic life.

Law 12
Offer Generosity

Generosity is a powerful tool for building strong relationships, enhancing reputation, and attracting opportunities. Generous acts create a cycle of reciprocity that benefits both the giver and the recipient, fostering trust, admiration, and a mutual support network. Studies show that practicing generosity not only improves well-being but also cultivates qualities like empathy and gratitude, essential for personal and emotional growth.

By sharing resources, time, or knowledge, you expand your influence and build connections based on trust and respect. Small acts of kindness in daily life or providing support during crucial moments can strengthen bonds and solidify partnerships. Moreover, strategic generosity that genuinely addresses real needs maximizes your ability to engage and inspire others.

Practicing generosity requires balance. Setting healthy boundaries protects against exploitation and ensures your actions remain effective and meaningful. Incorporating generosity into your routine and using it as a tool to strengthen interpersonal bonds allows you to transform everyday interactions into opportunities to create a positive and lasting impact.

Generosity is one of the cornerstones of modern power. It is not merely an expression of altruism but also a pathway to achieving tangible results in your personal and professional life. By applying it strategically and genuinely, you build a solid foundation for thriving in any sphere.

Personal Benefits:

Strengthening bonds: Generosity creates a virtuous cycle of reciprocity, reinforcing your connections with those around you and building a mutual support network.

Increasing influence: Generous acts enhance your influence over others, as people naturally feel inclined to reciprocate kindness and cooperate with those who help them.

Improving reputation: Generosity helps build a positive reputation, conveying an image of altruism, compassion, and leadership.

Attracting opportunities: Generous individuals attract opportunities, as they inspire trust, admiration, and goodwill in others.

Boosting happiness: Studies show that generosity increases happiness and well-being for both the giver and the recipient.

Personal growth: Practicing generosity fosters qualities like empathy, compassion, and gratitude, contributing to your personal and emotional development.

Methods of Application:

Offer your time and skills:

Volunteering: Dedicate your time to social causes or organizations you believe in, using your skills and knowledge to help others.

Mentorship: Share your experience and expertise with individuals starting their careers or seeking guidance in life.

Supporting friends and family: Be available to assist your loved ones in times of need, offering both practical and emotional support.

Share your resources:

Donations: Contribute financially to social causes or charitable institutions you support.

Knowledge sharing: Freely share your knowledge and ideas, contributing to others' learning and growth.

Material resources: Share material possessions that may be useful to others with generosity.

Practice generosity in daily life:

Small acts of kindness: Engage in small acts of kindness, such as helping a stranger, giving up your seat on the bus, or complimenting someone.

Active listening: Be available to listen to those who need to vent or share concerns, offering empathy and compassion.

Forgiveness: Practice forgiveness by releasing grudges and offering second chances to those who have wronged you.

Be strategic in your generosity:

Identify others' needs: Pay attention to the needs of those around you and offer help in a genuine and relevant way.

Offer help without expecting anything in return: True generosity is selfless. Provide assistance without seeking immediate reciprocity or recognition.

Build relationships through generosity: Use generosity to establish strong, lasting relationships based on trust and mutual support.

Step-by-Step Guide to Applying the Law "Offer Generosity":

Identify your skills and resources: Recognize the talents, knowledge, and resources you can share with others.

Find opportunities to be generous: Look for ways to practice generosity within your community, work, or personal life.

Offer genuine and relevant help: Pay attention to others' needs and provide assistance that is truly helpful and meaningful.

Practice daily generosity: Incorporate generosity into your daily habits, performing small acts of kindness and offering support to others.

Build relationships through generosity: Use generosity to strengthen your connections with those around you and create a mutual support network.

Adjustments If Expected Results Do Not Occur:

If you feel exploited: Reassess your boundaries and learn to say "no" when necessary to prevent your generosity from being misused.

If you don't receive recognition: Remember that true generosity is selfless. Focus on the satisfaction of helping others, rather than seeking external acknowledgment.

If you don't feel like you're making a difference: Explore new ways to contribute and find causes that genuinely inspire you to be generous.

Examples:

A leader mentoring team members: Shares knowledge and experience, helping them develop their skills and achieve their goals.

A businessperson donating a portion of profits to charity: Contributes to a social cause while strengthening the company's image.

A friend offering emotional support during tough times: Demonstrates compassion and strengthens friendship bonds.

When practiced genuinely and strategically, generosity is not only an act of altruism but also a skill that enhances human connections, strengthens your position in interpersonal relationships, and promotes mutual growth. By offering resources, time, and support, you build a network of trust and reciprocity that amplifies your influence and solidifies your reputation. Generosity is a transformative tool: it attracts opportunities, improves your quality of life, and creates positive impacts around you, enabling you to wield power with empathy, balance, and purpose.

Law 13
Disarm Opposition

Disarming opposition is an essential skill for achieving strategic outcomes and preserving your energy in a world filled with conflict. By intelligently and constructively neutralizing opponents, you avoid unnecessary strain, safeguard your interests, and simultaneously strengthen your position while opening doors to new opportunities. Studies in human behavior and conflict resolution show that understanding others' motivations and adopting diplomatic approaches are effective methods for transforming adversaries into allies and fostering mutual growth.

Handling opposition strategically reduces friction, protects your reputation, and demonstrates confidence and resilience. Techniques such as analyzing opponents' intentions and vulnerabilities, engaging in dialogue, and employing creative strategies like humor or forming alliances enhance your ability to influence and manage challenging situations. Beyond avoiding confrontation, this approach fosters inner peace and emotional well-being, creating a virtuous cycle of stability and progress.

Personal Benefits:

Conflict reduction: Disarming opposition helps avoid unnecessary conflicts, preserving your energy and protecting your reputation.

Protection against attacks: Neutralizing opponents prevents them from undermining your interests or sabotaging your plans.

Opportunity creation: Turning enemies into allies opens doors to new opportunities for collaboration and growth.

Position strengthening: Demonstrating the ability to handle opposition reinforces your position and increases your influence.

Confidence building: Overcoming challenges and neutralizing opponents boosts self-confidence and resilience.

Inner peace promotion: Constructively addressing opposition contributes to inner peace and emotional well-being.

Methods of Application:

Understand your opponents:

Identify their motivations: Seek to understand the reasons behind their opposition. What drives them to oppose you? What are their interests and goals?

Analyze their strengths and weaknesses: Evaluate their strong points and vulnerabilities to develop effective strategies to neutralize them.

Build empathy: Try to put yourself in their position and understand their perspectives, even if you disagree with them.

Use diplomacy and negotiation:

Seek dialogue: Open a communication channel with opponents and try to resolve disagreements peacefully and constructively.

Be open to concessions: Be willing to compromise on certain points to reach a mutually acceptable agreement.

Find common ground: Focus on shared interests and work toward solutions that benefit all parties.

Neutralize opposition with creative strategies:

Use humor: Humor can be a powerful tool to disarm opposition and create a lighter, more receptive atmosphere.

Change the game: If the current approach isn't working, change tactics and surprise your opponents with an unexpected strategy.

Form alliances: Gain the support of others to strengthen your position and isolate opponents.

Turn enemies into allies:

Show respect: Even if you disagree with them, treat opponents with respect and dignity.

Identify areas of cooperation: Look for opportunities to collaborate and work together toward a common goal.

Build bridges: Make small gestures of reconciliation and goodwill to pave the way for a more positive relationship.

Step-by-Step Guide to Applying the Law "Disarm Opposition":

Understand your opponents: Identify their motivations, strengths, and weaknesses.

Use diplomacy: Engage in dialogue, remain open to concessions, and find common ground.

Neutralize opposition: Use humor, shift strategies, and form alliances.

Turn enemies into allies: Show respect, find areas for cooperation, and build bridges.

Adjustments If Expected Results Do Not Occur:

If opposition persists: Reassess your strategy and explore new ways to neutralize opponents.

If you feel threatened or intimidated: Seek the support of trusted individuals or appropriate authorities.

If the situation becomes unsustainable: Remove yourself from the conflict and look for new opportunities.

Examples:

A politician seeking support from a rival: Publicly praises their qualities and proposes an alliance around a mutually beneficial project.

A manager facing team resistance: Organizes a meeting to hear employees' concerns and collaboratively find solutions.

A student experiencing bullying at school: Speaks with parents and teachers, enlists friends' support, and develops strategies to assertively address the situation.

Disarming opposition is not merely a way to handle challenges but a path to strengthening your position and building relationships based on respect and cooperation. By understanding opponents' motivations and adopting a diplomatic and creative approach, you turn conflicts into growth opportunities. Transforming enemies into allies not only minimizes obstacles but also expands your support network and establishes a solid foundation for achieving broader objectives. When applied consistently and intelligently, this law becomes a powerful tool for anyone seeking to wield influence and achieve sustainable success.

Law 14
Build Networks

Building networks is one of the most impactful skills for achieving personal and professional success today. A strong network not only connects you to opportunities but also broadens your access to information, provides support during critical moments, and enhances your visibility. Authentic and strategic relationships transform contacts into allies, fostering collaboration, growth, and progress in any field of endeavor.

Networks are not just a mechanism of exchange but an asset that multiplies your reach and influence. By identifying key people, building genuine ties, and strengthening connections, you create a foundation of support that inspires trust and drives progress. Over time, this approach enhances your self-confidence and strengthens your ability to achieve goals more effectively and strategically.

Personal Advantages:

Expanding opportunities: A strong network opens doors to new business opportunities, jobs, partnerships, and collaborations.

Access to information: Your network can provide valuable insights into market trends, competitors, potential clients, and other relevant information for your success.

Support and collaboration: A diverse network offers support in various areas, such as mentorship, advice, feedback, and assistance in times of difficulty.

Increased visibility: Your network can help boost your visibility and recognition in your field of expertise.

Personal and professional development: Interacting with people from different backgrounds and experiences fosters personal and professional growth.

Boosting self-confidence: Building a strong network increases your confidence and belief in your ability to achieve your goals.

Methods of Application:

1. Identify Key People:

Map your current network: Start by identifying the people already in your network and analyze their strengths and weaknesses.

Define your targets: Determine the individuals you want to include in your network, considering your goals and needs.

Attend strategic events: Participate in relevant events and conferences in your field, where you can meet influential people and make new contacts.

2. Build Authentic Relationships:

Be genuine and interested: Show genuine interest in people, their stories, and their goals.

Offer help and support: Be willing to assist others by sharing your knowledge, resources, and contacts.

Maintain regular contact: Stay in touch with the people in your network, even when there is no immediate need.

3. Strengthen Your Ties:

Create emotional connections: Share personal experiences, demonstrate vulnerability, and build emotional bonds with the people in your network.

Find common interests: Identify shared interests with people in your network and promote activities that strengthen these ties.

Be a good listener: Pay attention to what people have to say and show empathy and understanding.

4. Use Your Network Strategically:

Ask for help when needed: Don't hesitate to seek support or guidance from your network.

Connect people: Introduce individuals in your network who can mutually benefit from each other, creating a virtuous cycle of collaboration.

Reciprocate generosity: Always be willing to return the help you receive, maintaining balance in relationships and strengthening your reputation.

Step-by-Step Guide to Applying the "Build Networks" Law:

Identify key people: Map your current network, define your targets, and attend strategic events.

Build authentic relationships: Be genuine, show interest, and offer help.

Strengthen your ties: Create emotional connections, find common interests, and be a good listener.

Use your network strategically: Ask for help, connect people, and reciprocate generosity.

Adjustments if the Expected Outcome Does Not Occur:

If you struggle to make new contacts: Practice your social skills, prepare a concise and effective "elevator pitch," and seek opportunities to interact with new people.

If your relationships are superficial: Invest time and energy in cultivating your ties, sharing personal experiences, and showing genuine interest in others.

If you are not getting the expected benefits from your network: Review your networking strategy, identify more relevant people for your goals, and focus on building stronger and more strategic relationships.

Examples:

A professional seeking a new job opportunity: Contacts people in their network for referrals, attends networking events, and uses LinkedIn to connect with professionals in their field.

An entrepreneur looking for investors for their business: Presents their project to influential people in their network, seeks mentorship from experienced entrepreneurs, and attends startup events.

An artist wanting to showcase their work: Shares their creations with influential people on social media, organizes exhibitions, and seeks partnerships with galleries and curators.

Building networks is an art that requires time, dedication, and skill. By identifying key people, cultivating authentic relationships, and using your network strategically, you create a virtuous circle of connections that drives personal and professional growth. Remember, success is not an individual game. Build a strong network, and you will reap the rewards of collaboration, mutual support, and the endless possibilities that arise when people unite around common goals.

Law 15
Master Information

Mastering information is an indispensable skill for achieving goals and thriving in a competitive environment. Accurate and relevant information strengthens decision-making, anticipates trends, and reveals opportunities that might otherwise go unnoticed. Furthermore, understanding and organizing data strategically enhances communication, boosts credibility, and fosters personal and professional growth.

Access to information is merely the first step; the true power lies in the ability to analyze, interpret, and use it effectively. When well-managed, information becomes a strategic advantage that drives success in any field. This practice not only promotes individual development but also contributes to building a more informed, reliable, and productive environment.

Personal Advantages:

More effective decision-making: Accurate and relevant information enables better decisions, reducing risks and increasing chances of success.

Anticipating trends: Mastering information allows you to identify emerging trends and prepare for the future, ensuring relevance and competitiveness.

Identifying opportunities: Information is key to discovering new business, investment, partnership, and growth opportunities.

Improving communication: Mastering information helps you communicate more clearly, accurately, and persuasively.

Increasing credibility: Being a reliable source of information enhances your credibility and influence in your field.

Personal and professional growth: The constant pursuit of knowledge and information fosters growth, paving the way for success.

Methods of Application:

1. Develop Research Skills:

Reliable sources: Learn to identify trustworthy information sources, such as academic publications, reputable news sites, and recognized experts.

Research techniques: Master effective research techniques, such as using keywords, search filters, and social media monitoring tools.

Critical thinking: Develop critical thinking to evaluate the validity and relevance of the information you find.

2. Master the Art of Analysis:

Organizing information: Arrange the information you collect clearly and structurally, using tools like mind maps, charts, and tables.

Identifying patterns: Look for patterns and trends in the information you analyze, drawing relevant insights and conclusions.

Interpreting and synthesizing: Interpret data and synthesize information into clear, concise conclusions for decision-making.

3. Manage Knowledge:

Create an organizational system: Efficiently organize your files, notes, and other materials so you can easily access them when needed.

Share knowledge: Share information and insights with others, contributing to collective learning and strengthening your network.

Stay updated: Keep yourself informed about the latest news, trends, and developments in your area of expertise.

4. Protect Information:

Information security: Safeguard your confidential information against unauthorized access using strong passwords, encryption, and other security measures.

Privacy: Respect people's privacy and refrain from sharing confidential information without authorization.

Fact-checking: Verify the accuracy of information before sharing it, avoiding the spread of fake news and misinformation.

Step-by-Step Guide to Applying the "Master Information" Law:

Develop research skills: Seek reliable sources, master research techniques, and hone critical thinking.

Master the art of analysis: Organize information, identify patterns, and interpret data.

Manage knowledge: Create an organizational system, share knowledge, and stay updated.

Protect information: Ensure information security, respect privacy, and verify facts.

Adjustments if the Expected Outcome Does Not Occur:

If you have difficulty finding relevant information: Redefine your research strategies, seek alternative sources, and use more advanced monitoring tools.

If you feel overwhelmed by the volume of information: Use filtering and prioritization tools, focus on the most important information, and learn to delegate research tasks.

If you struggle to interpret data: Seek help from experts, use data visualization tools, and improve your analytical skills.

Examples:

An investor seeking opportunities in the financial market: Analyzes economic data, follows market news, and monitors company performance.

A scientist conducting new research: Completes a comprehensive literature review, collects experimental data, and rigorously analyzes the results.

A journalist writing an investigative report: Gathers information from various sources, interviews key people, and carefully fact-checks.

Mastering information is an essential skill for success in an increasingly complex and dynamic world. By developing research skills, critical analysis, and knowledge management, you become a more effective decision-maker, a more competitive professional, and a more informed and conscious individual. Remember, information is power. Master it and use it to your advantage.

Lei 16
Crie Urgência

Criar urgência é uma estratégia poderosa para acelerar decisões, mobilizar pessoas e alcançar resultados em um ambiente cada vez mais dinâmico e competitivo. Ao utilizar gatilhos psicológicos como escassez, prova social e medo da perda, é possível inspirar ação imediata e evitar a procrastinação. Essa habilidade é essencial para liderar com eficiência, gerenciar crises e maximizar a produtividade em projetos e negociações.

A urgência não é apenas uma ferramenta de pressão, mas um meio eficaz de alinhar objetivos e motivar ações em tempo hábil. Comunicar limites claros, estabelecer prazos específicos e reforçar o valor de agir rapidamente são práticas que fortalecem sua influência e elevam sua capacidade de atingir metas de forma consistente. Quando utilizada de forma ética e com propósito, a urgência transforma desafios em oportunidades concretas.

Vantagens Pessoais:

Aceleração de decisões: A urgência estimula a tomada de decisão, evitando procrastinação e impulsionando a ação.

Aumento da conversão: Em vendas e negociações, a urgência aumenta as taxas de conversão, levando os clientes a fecharem negócios mais rapidamente.

Mobilização de pessoas: A urgência é uma ferramenta poderosa para mobilizar pessoas em torno de uma causa ou objetivo, inspirando ação coletiva e engajamento.

Melhoria da produtividade: Criar urgência em tarefas e projetos aumenta a produtividade, evitando atrasos e garantindo que os prazos sejam cumpridos.

Fortalecimento da liderança: Líderes que sabem criar urgência inspiram ação e motivam suas equipes a alcançar resultados extraordinários.

Gerenciamento de crises: Em situações de crise, a urgência é essencial para tomar decisões rápidas e eficazes, minimizando danos e resolvendo problemas com agilidade.

Métodos de Aplicação:

1. Utilize gatilhos psicológicos:

Escassez: A percepção de escassez cria urgência, pois as pessoas temem perder uma oportunidade única. Exemplos: "vagas limitadas", "oferta por tempo limitado", "edição exclusiva".

Prova social: Mostrar que outras pessoas estão aproveitando a oportunidade cria urgência por meio da influência social. Exemplos: "mais de 1000 pessoas já compraram", "produto mais vendido", "recomendado por especialistas".

Medo da perda: Enfatizar as consequências negativas de não agir rapidamente cria urgência pelo medo da perda. Exemplos: "não perca esta chance", "última oportunidade", "preços vão aumentar".

2. Comunique a urgência de forma eficaz:

Linguagem persuasiva: Utilize palavras e expressões que transmitam urgência, como "agora", "imediatamente", "urgente", "não perca tempo".

Tom de voz: Utilize um tom de voz enérgico e convincente para reforçar a mensagem de urgência.

Comunicação não-verbal: Utilize expressões faciais e linguagem corporal que transmitam entusiasmo e ação.

3. Crie prazos e limites:

Defina prazos claros: Estabeleça prazos específicos para a tomada de decisão ou ação, criando um senso de limite e escassez.

Ofereça bônus por tempo limitado: Incentive a ação imediata oferecendo bônus ou vantagens exclusivas para quem agir dentro do prazo estabelecido.

Crie gatilhos visuais: Utilize cronômetros, contagens regressivas ou outros gatilhos visuais para reforçar a sensação de urgência.

4. Utilize a urgência com ética:

Seja honesto e transparente: Não crie falsa urgência ou utilize táticas manipulativas para pressionar as pessoas.

Ofereça valor real: Garanta que a oportunidade que você está oferecendo é realmente valiosa e relevante para o público.

Respeite os limites das pessoas: Não seja insistente ou agressivo em sua abordagem. Dê às pessoas o tempo e o espaço necessários para tomarem suas decisões.

Guia Passo a Passo para Aplicar a Lei "Crie Urgência":

1 - Defina seu objetivo: Determine o que você deseja alcançar criando urgência (ex: aumentar vendas, acelerar decisões, mobilizar pessoas).

2 - Identifique seu público: Conheça as necessidades, desejos e motivações do seu público-alvo.

3 - Escolha os gatilhos psicológicos adequados: Utilize gatilhos como escassez, prova social e medo da perda para criar urgência.

4 - Comunique a urgência de forma eficaz: Utilize linguagem persuasiva, tom de voz e comunicação não-verbal para reforçar a mensagem.

5 - Crie prazos e limites: Estabeleça prazos claros, ofereça bônus por tempo limitado e utilize gatilhos visuais.

Ajustes caso o Resultado Esperado não Ocorra:

Se a urgência não estiver motivando a ação: Revise sua estratégia, experimente diferentes gatilhos psicológicos e adapte sua comunicação.

Se as pessoas se sentirem pressionadas: Ajuste seu tom de voz e linguagem, garantindo que você não esteja sendo manipulativo ou agressivo.

Se a urgência não for percebida como genuína: Reforce a veracidade da sua mensagem, apresentando provas e evidências que justifiquem a urgência.

Exemplos:

Uma loja online que oferece descontos exclusivos por 24 horas: Cria urgência utilizando o gatilho da escassez e do prazo limitado.

Um líder que convoca uma reunião de emergência para discutir uma crise: Cria urgência pela importância e gravidade da situação.

Um profissional de marketing que utiliza o gatilho da prova social em uma campanha publicitária: Exibe depoimentos de clientes satisfeitos para incentivar a compra do produto.

A criação de urgência, quando aplicada com sabedoria, é uma das estratégias mais eficazes para transformar intenções em ações. Seja para aumentar vendas, liderar equipes ou gerenciar crises, a urgência é uma força que impulsiona resultados rápidos e significativos. Ao incorporar essa prática em sua abordagem, você não apenas inspira agilidade, mas também fortalece sua posição como líder eficaz e estrategista hábil, capaz de mobilizar recursos e alcançar objetivos com precisão e propósito.

Law 17
Master the Art of Negotiation

    The art of negotiation is one of the most powerful skills a person can develop in life. In a world driven by social interactions and diverse interests, mastering negotiation is not just an advantage but a necessity for achieving success in multiple spheres. From the professional seeking a fairer salary to the diplomat negotiating peace treaties, the ability to understand the other side, present persuasive arguments, and find mutually beneficial solutions distinguishes an effective negotiator from an amateur.

    Negotiation is not just about winning but about building. The most impactful results come from negotiations that strengthen relationships, build trust, and open doors for future collaborations. Every step, from careful preparation to closing the deal, requires a combination of practical skills, such as research and strategy, and interpersonal qualities, such as empathy and clear communication.

    Additionally, negotiation is a powerful tool for resolving conflicts constructively. It transforms disputes into opportunities for cooperation and allows different parties to find common ground. When well-conducted, the process also serves as a platform to expand influence, demonstrate leadership, and create value both individually and collectively.

    Therefore, mastering negotiation is not just about securing better deals; it is about evolving personally and professionally. It's about being strategic, persuasive, and empathetic simultaneously. When you take control of your interactions with others and become an excellent negotiator, you unlock a world of possibilities where positive outcomes and lasting relationships coexist harmoniously.

Personal Benefits:

Better outcomes: Masterful negotiation enables you to achieve more favorable results in any situation—professional, personal, or social.

Relationship building: Successful negotiations strengthen relationships, fostering trust and cooperation.

Conflict resolution: Negotiation is a powerful tool for resolving conflicts constructively, finding solutions that meet all parties' interests.

Increased influence: Skilled negotiators wield greater influence, persuading and motivating others to accept their ideas and proposals.

Personal and professional development: Mastering negotiation enhances personal and professional growth.

Value creation: Effective negotiations generate value for all parties involved, delivering positive results and mutual benefits.

Application Methods:

Prepare for the negotiation:

Define your objectives: Be clear about your goals and what you aim to achieve during the negotiation.

Know the other party: Research the other party, their interests, needs, and negotiation style.

Develop a strategy: Plan your approach, anticipate possible objections, and craft persuasive arguments.

Build rapport:

Establish connection: Build a genuine connection with the other party by demonstrating empathy, respect, and interest in their goals.

Communicate clearly: Express your ideas concisely and persuasively, using language the other party understands.

Listen actively: Pay attention to what the other party says, ask questions, and show that you value their opinions.

Master persuasion techniques:

Provide evidence and proof: Support your arguments with data, statistics, examples, and testimonials that highlight the value of your proposal.

Use storytelling: Tell compelling stories that resonate emotionally with the other party to strengthen your case.

Appeal to reciprocity: Make small concessions to encourage the other party to reciprocate by yielding on their points.

Handle objections effectively:

Listen attentively to objections: Do not interrupt and seek to understand the reasoning behind their objections.

Respond with empathy: Acknowledge their concerns and demonstrate understanding of their perspective.

Offer alternative solutions: Be prepared to present alternative solutions that address their needs and benefit you.

Close the negotiation masterfully:

Formalize the agreement: Document the agreement terms clearly to prevent future misunderstandings.

Celebrate success: Acknowledge the efforts of all parties involved and celebrate the agreement reached.

Maintain the relationship: Continue nurturing the relationship with the other party post-negotiation to build a solid foundation for future interactions.

Step-by-Step Guide to Applying the "Master the Art of Negotiation" Principle:

Prepare for the negotiation: Define your goals, understand the other party, and create a strategy.

Build rapport: Establish connection, communicate effectively, and listen actively.

Master persuasion techniques: Present evidence, use storytelling, and appeal to reciprocity.

Handle objections: Listen attentively, respond empathetically, and offer alternative solutions.

Close with mastery: Formalize the agreement, celebrate success, and maintain the relationship.

Adjustments if Desired Results Are Not Achieved:

If you fail to reach an agreement: Reevaluate your strategy, seek new information, and be open to making further concessions.

If you feel pressured or intimidated: Stay calm, assert your interests firmly, and do not hesitate to withdraw from the negotiation if necessary.

If the agreement is not honored: Document breaches of the agreement and explore legal avenues to enforce your rights.

Examples:

A professional negotiating a salary increase: Presents their achievements and demonstrates their value to the company, arguing persuasively for a mutually beneficial agreement.

A couple negotiating household task division: Openly discusses their needs and expectations, aiming for a fair and balanced solution that satisfies both parties.

A diplomat negotiating a peace treaty between two nations: Employs diplomacy and persuasion to build bridges of understanding and achieve an agreement that fosters peace and cooperation.

Mastering negotiation is a journey combining preparation, strategic communication, and the ability to address challenges constructively. Every successful negotiation represents not just a step toward your goals but also an opportunity to strengthen relationships and solidify your reputation as a trustworthy and influential individual.

Remember, negotiation does not end with the formalization of an agreement; it continues with maintaining the relationships built. By celebrating achieved results and nurturing your connection with the other party, you create a solid base for future collaborations and opportunities.

Mastering the art of negotiation is not a final destination but an ongoing process of learning and adaptation. With practice, persistence, and a focus on creating value for all parties, you will achieve superior results and become a change agent capable of positively influencing people and the environment around you.

May every interaction be an opportunity to showcase your mastery and create a lasting impact.

Law 18
Lead Change

Leading change is an essential skill for anyone seeking to stand out in a constantly evolving world. In a landscape where adaptability is key to survival, those who view change as an opportunity rather than a threat have a significant competitive edge. Leading change goes beyond merely adjusting to new conditions; it involves influencing people, motivating them to adapt, and guiding organizations to achieve superior results amidst uncertainty.

By leading change, you cultivate attributes such as resilience, creativity, and self-confidence while creating a positive impact on your environment. This process enables you to uncover hidden potential in people and systems, driving innovation and promoting growth. However, resistance to change is a natural challenge stemming from insecurities, fears, or even a lack of vision. A true leader is one who, with empathy and strategy, can overcome these barriers, inspire trust, and chart a clear path forward.

Each stage of the change process requires specific skills: from adopting an open and positive mindset to effectively communicating the benefits of transformation. Leadership by example is particularly powerful as it demonstrates commitment and encourages others to follow the same path.

Leading change not only transforms organizations but also strengthens your ability to navigate personal challenges. It is a journey of continuous learning, where the rewards include both tangible results and the personal and collective growth generated along the way.

Personal Benefits:

Adaptability and resilience: Leading change develops your adaptability and resilience, enabling you to navigate complex and uncertain environments with greater confidence and flexibility.

Growth and innovation: Change drives growth and innovation, paving the way for new ideas, processes, and solutions.

Opportunities: Change creates new opportunities for those prepared to embrace and lead it.

Influence and leadership: Leading change strengthens your leadership, inspiring and motivating people to follow your vision and adapt to new realities.

Performance improvement: Adapting to change can lead to significant improvements in individual and organizational performance.

Increased self-confidence: Overcoming the challenges of change boosts your self-confidence and belief in your ability to handle adversity.

Application Methods:

Embrace change:

Shift your mindset: Cultivate an open and positive attitude toward change, viewing it as an opportunity for growth and improvement.

Adapt quickly: Enhance your ability to adjust plans and strategies as circumstances evolve.

Step out of your comfort zone: Be willing to try new things, challenge your beliefs, and explore uncharted territories.

Inspire and motivate people:

Communicate the vision: Share your vision for the future and explain how the proposed changes will contribute to achieving it.

Connect emotionally: Present the benefits of change clearly and compellingly, resonating with people's emotions and aspirations.

Lead by example: Demonstrate your commitment to change by embracing it with enthusiasm and positivity.

Overcome resistance:

Identify the causes of resistance: Understand why people resist change, whether it stems from fear of the unknown, insecurity, or attachment to the past.

Communicate openly: Foster an environment of open and honest dialogue where people feel comfortable expressing their concerns and doubts.

Provide support and training: Equip people with the necessary support and training to feel confident and prepared to handle change.

Manage the change process:

Set clear goals and objectives: Define clear goals for the change process, ensuring everyone aligns with the desired direction.

Implement changes gradually: Introduce changes in a structured and phased manner, allowing people to adjust to the new pace and routines.

Monitor progress and make adjustments: Track the progress of change, evaluate outcomes, and make necessary adjustments along the way.

Step-by-Step Guide to Applying the "Lead Change" Principle:

Embrace change: Shift your mindset, adapt with agility, and step out of your comfort zone.

Inspire people: Communicate the vision, connect emotionally, and lead by example.

Overcome resistance: Identify its causes, communicate openly, and provide support.

Manage the process: Set clear goals, implement changes gradually, and monitor progress.

Adjustments if Desired Results Are Not Achieved:

If resistance to change is too strong: Strengthen communication, foster dialogue, and seek the support of informal leaders to influence the group.

If the change process is too slow: Accelerate implementation without compromising quality or people's adaptation.

If results are not as expected: Revise goals, adjust strategies, and explore new ways to motivate and engage people.

Examples:

A CEO leading a company's digital transformation: Implements new technologies, invests in training, and motivates employees to embrace a new digital culture.

A teacher adopting new teaching methodologies: Demonstrates the advantages of the new approach, provides support to students, and adapts lesson plans to meet class needs.

A community leader mobilizing neighbors for a neighborhood revitalization project: Shares a vision of a safer, more beautiful neighborhood, organizes meetings, and encourages everyone's participation.

Leading change is more than adapting to a new landscape; it is influencing, inspiring, and guiding others toward a more promising future. This process demands courage, vision, and empathy but offers invaluable rewards for those who commit to it.

By overcoming resistance, communicating clearly, and implementing changes gradually, you not only facilitate the transition but also create an environment of trust and collaboration. Remember, every challenge faced along the way is an opportunity for growth and strengthening, both for yourself and those who accompany you.

Change is inevitable, but how you lead it determines its impact on your surroundings. Seize every opportunity to lead with purpose and integrity, creating a legacy of innovation and resilience. With determination and skill, you can transform uncertainties into possibilities and build a future aligned with your vision and the aspirations of those around you.

Law 19
Build Alliances

Building alliances is an essential strategy for achieving ambitious goals and overcoming challenges in a competitive and ever-changing environment. From business partnerships to international collaborations, alliances are powerful tools for amplifying resources, sharing responsibilities, and opening doors to new opportunities.

A successful alliance transcends merely joining forces; it creates synergy, where the whole is greater than the sum of its parts. Through strategic partnerships, you can access untapped markets, accelerate growth, and innovate meaningfully. Alliances also allow for shared risk, providing greater security and resilience in complex endeavors. However, success in this process depends on identifying the right partners, cultivating trust, and managing collaboration effectively.

Building alliances is not just about technical or operational matters—it requires a shared vision, aligned values, and open, transparent communication. Trust is the cornerstone of any enduring partnership and is built through consistent actions, keeping commitments, and continuous effort to strengthen personal and professional ties.

Mastering the art of forging alliances is a skill that transforms not only the trajectory of a project or organization but also personal growth. Knowing how to unite efforts with others and leveraging each party's strengths enables you to tackle adversities strategically and effectively. In a world where no one succeeds alone, alliances pave the way for sustainable and impactful achievements.

Personal Benefits:

Resource amplification: Alliances grant access to resources otherwise unavailable, such as technology, capital, expertise, and networks.

Market expansion: Strategic alliances can open doors to new markets, increasing reach and customer base.

Risk reduction: Sharing risks with partners minimizes exposure to losses and enhances the chances of success in risky ventures.

Increased competitiveness: Alliances strengthen your competitive position, enabling you to face larger and more powerful competitors.

Accelerated growth: Partnerships can speed up growth, helping you achieve your goals more quickly and efficiently.

Innovation: Collaboration with partners fosters innovation, generating new ideas, products, and services.

Application Methods:

Identify ideal partners:

Define your needs: Analyze your strengths and weaknesses to identify areas where you need support and complementation.

Seek complementarity: Look for partners with skills, resources, and experiences that complement yours.

Share values: Choose partners who share your values and future vision.

Negotiate mutually beneficial agreements:

Clearly define terms: Establish clear terms for the alliance, including objectives, responsibilities, shared resources, and the division of benefits.

Be flexible and open to concessions: Be willing to negotiate and make concessions to reach a fair and beneficial agreement for all parties.

Formalize the agreement: Document the terms of the alliance in a formal contract to ensure security and adherence to commitments.

Cultivate trust:

Communicate openly and transparently: Maintain open and honest communication with your partners, sharing relevant information and keeping them updated on the alliance's progress.

Keep your commitments: Demonstrate reliability by fulfilling your obligations with integrity and responsibility.

Build personal relationships: Invest time in getting to know your partners personally, fostering bonds of friendship and trust.

Manage the alliance effectively:

Set common goals and objectives: Establish clear goals and objectives for the alliance to ensure alignment and collaboration.

Monitor progress and outcomes: Track the alliance's progress, evaluate results, and make necessary adjustments to ensure success.

Celebrate successes and learn from mistakes: Acknowledge and celebrate achievements and use errors as opportunities for learning and improvement.

Step-by-Step Guide to Applying the "Build Alliances" Principle:

Identify ideal partners: Define your needs, seek complementarity, and share values.

Negotiate mutually beneficial agreements: Define terms, be flexible, and formalize the agreement.

Cultivate trust: Communicate openly, keep commitments, and build personal relationships.

Manage the alliance: Set common goals, monitor progress, and celebrate successes.

Adjustments if Desired Results Are Not Achieved:

If you struggle to find suitable partners: Expand your network, attend industry events, and seek help from consultants specializing in strategic alliances.

If the alliance does not yield expected results: Review the agreement terms, renegotiate responsibilities, and address any issues hindering the partnership's success.

If conflicts or trust issues arise: Promote dialogue, involve a mediator, and emphasize transparent communication and commitment.

Examples:

Two companies collaborating to develop a new product: They share technological knowledge, invest in research and development, and launch the product together, splitting costs and profits.

A freelancer teaming up with other professionals to create a multidisciplinary clinic: They share physical space, operational costs, and clientele, offering more comprehensive services and attracting a larger audience.

Two countries forming a military alliance to defend against a common enemy: They share military resources, develop joint strategies, and support each other in case of conflict.

Alliances are a cornerstone for success in any endeavor, enabling achievements that would be impossible alone. Combining diverse resources, experiences, and visions fosters an environment ripe for innovation, accelerated growth, and market competitiveness.

Like any relationship, alliances require dedication, trust, and skill to thrive. From carefully choosing partners to celebrating shared successes, every step of the process must be guided by transparency, commitment, and clearly aligned goals.

By cultivating strategic alliances, you not only expand your capabilities but also strengthen your support network and open doors to new collaborations and learning opportunities. Remember, building alliances is not just about achieving immediate goals—it's about establishing connections that can bear fruit for years to come. With focus, strategy, and empathy, you can transform each partnership into a pathway to mutual success.

Law 20
Manage Time

Effective time management is one of the most valuable skills anyone can acquire. In a world where demands seem to grow continuously, knowing how to organize and prioritize your activities can be the difference between success and failure, balance and burnout. Mastering the art of time management not only boosts your productivity but also enhances your quality of life, reduces stress, and creates space for what truly matters.

Time is a finite resource, and every wasted minute is a missed opportunity to move closer to your goals. Planning your routine, eliminating distractions, and optimizing activities are essential steps to ensure you use this resource wisely and strategically. By adopting practices such as using organizational tools, delegating tasks, and cultivating healthy habits, you can transform your routine and achieve performance levels you once thought unattainable.

More than just productivity, time management is about self-discipline and clarity of purpose. It requires honest analysis of your priorities and a commitment to align your actions with what truly matters. Whether you are a student preparing for a major exam, a professional striving for career growth, or someone seeking to balance work and personal life, time management benefits everyone, regardless of their field.

Personal Advantages:

Increased Productivity: Effective time management helps you accomplish more in less time, boosting productivity and efficiency.

Reduced Stress: Organizing and prioritizing tasks lowers stress and anxiety, allowing you to focus on what's truly important.

Improved Quality of Life: Managing time frees up hours for enjoyable activities, such as family time, exercise, and hobbies, enhancing overall well-being.

Goal Achievement: Prioritizing essential tasks increases your chances of achieving your objectives more quickly and efficiently.

Enhanced Organization: Time management helps you stay organized in all areas of life, from work responsibilities to household chores.

Increased Self-Discipline: Developing time management habits strengthens your self-discipline and ability to concentrate on priorities.

Methods of Application:

Plan Your Time:

Define Goals and Objectives: Start by setting short-, medium-, and long-term goals to clarify where you want to go and how you'll use your time to get there.

Create a Schedule: Use a calendar, app, or planner to organize your daily, weekly, and monthly tasks and commitments.

Prioritize Tasks: Use methods like the Eisenhower Matrix (urgent/important) to focus on activities that have the greatest impact.

Eliminate Distractions:

Identify Time Wasters: Analyze your routine and pinpoint habits or activities that drain your time, such as social media, excessive emails, or unnecessary meetings.

Create a Distraction-Free Environment: Arrange your workspace, turn off phone notifications, and set aside time to work in a calm, interruption-free setting.

Manage Your Energy: Schedule challenging tasks during peak energy hours, reserving lighter activities for times when your energy dips.

Optimize Your Routine:

Automate Tasks: Use tools and technology to automate repetitive tasks like bill payments, social media scheduling, and email management.

Delegate Responsibilities: Hand off tasks that don't require your direct attention, freeing up time for strategic activities.

Learn to Say "No": Decline commitments and requests that don't align with your priorities and goals.

Cultivate Healthy Habits:

Get Sufficient Sleep: Adequate rest is crucial for focus, productivity, and overall well-being.

Maintain a Balanced Diet: A healthy diet provides the energy and nutrients needed for optimal mental and physical performance.

Exercise Regularly: Physical activity enhances mood, concentration, and overall health.

Step-by-Step Guide to Applying the "Manage Time" Law:

Plan Your Time: Define goals, create a schedule, and prioritize tasks.

Eliminate Distractions: Identify time wasters, create a distraction-free environment, and manage your energy.

Optimize Your Routine: Automate tasks, delegate responsibilities, and learn to say "no."

Cultivate Healthy Habits: Get enough sleep, eat well, and exercise.

Adjustments if Expected Results Are Not Achieved:

Difficulty Following a Schedule: Review your plan, adjust your timing, and remain flexible with your routine.

Feeling Overwhelmed: Delegate tasks, ask for help, and simplify your life by cutting unnecessary commitments.

Struggling to Focus: Practice concentration techniques like mindfulness or meditation, and create a more conducive work environment.

Examples

A student preparing for university entrance exams: Creates a study schedule, eliminates distractions like social media, and allocates time for rest and relaxation.

A professional aiming to increase workplace productivity: Organizes tasks by priority, uses time management tools, and delegates tasks to team members.

An individual seeking more family time: Sets clear work boundaries, schedules family activities, and disconnects from technology during leisure hours.

Managing time is a continuous practice of personal and professional growth. By focusing on planning tasks, eliminating distractions, and optimizing routines, you invest in an irreplaceable resource: your life. Every well-used minute is a step closer to your goals and a boost to your overall well-being.

Cultivating healthy habits like adequate sleep and regular exercise ensures the energy and mental clarity needed to tackle daily challenges. Moreover, learning to say "no" to unproductive activities is an act of courage and wisdom, essential for maintaining focus on your priorities.

The journey to mastering time management may seem challenging at first, but the results are transformative. With discipline, planning, and a proactive mindset, you'll not only enhance productivity but also carve out more time for what truly matters: the people, moments, and dreams that give life meaning. Let every minute be used with purpose and intention, and let time management be your tool for a fuller, more balanced life.

Law 21
Delegate Tasks

Delegating tasks is one of the most powerful and strategic practices in an effective leader's repertoire. Instead of overburdening yourself with all responsibilities, delegation allows you to focus your energy on high-impact activities while developing and motivating your team. Although many see delegation as simply redistributing tasks, it is a reflection of mature and intelligent leadership that understands success is not built alone but through solid collaboration.

The ability to delegate not only increases your personal productivity but also strengthens the team around you. By entrusting others with significant responsibilities, you provide opportunities for learning and growth, fostering self-confidence and engagement. Furthermore, delegating tasks to those with the right skills improves the quality of results by leveraging specific talents you may not possess.

However, effective delegation requires planning, clarity, and communication. Identifying the right tasks to delegate, selecting the appropriate people, and providing detailed instructions are crucial steps to ensure the responsibility is understood and accepted. Additionally, tracking progress in a balanced way—without stifling the autonomy of those involved—is essential for maintaining an atmosphere of trust and productivity.

Delegation is not a sign of weakness but of wisdom. It acknowledges that success is achieved when everyone contributes their best. When applied well, delegation transforms the work dynamic, enabling both the leader and the team to reach new heights of efficiency, innovation, and accomplishment.

Personal Benefits:

Increased productivity: Delegating tasks frees up your time to focus on more strategic and high-impact activities, boosting your efficiency.

Reduced stress: Sharing the workload reduces stress and anxiety, promoting a healthier and more balanced life.

Team development: Delegation is an opportunity to build your team's skills and confidence, preparing them for greater responsibilities in the future.

Improved work quality: Assigning tasks to those with specific expertise enhances the quality of work and achieves superior results.

Increased motivation: Delegation shows trust in your team, boosting their motivation and engagement.

Stronger leadership: Effective delegation reflects strong and confident leadership that earns respect and admiration.

Application Methods:

Identify the right tasks to delegate:

Analyze your activities: List your tasks and responsibilities, identifying those that can be delegated to others.

Prioritize your activities: Focus on tasks that require your specific skills and knowledge, delegating others.

Consider time and complexity: Delegate time-consuming or complex tasks so you can dedicate yourself to more critical activities.

Choose the right people for the tasks:

Evaluate skills and experience: Select individuals with the necessary skills and experience to execute the tasks effectively.

Consider availability and workload: Ensure selected individuals have the time and capacity to dedicate to the delegated tasks.

Provide development opportunities: Delegate tasks that challenge and help your team members develop their skills.

Provide clear and concise instructions:

Explain the task's objective: Clearly communicate the task's purpose and its importance to the project or organization.

Set expectations: Define expectations regarding outcomes, deadlines, and work quality.

Provide necessary resources: Ensure individuals have access to the tools, information, and materials required to complete the task.

Track progress and offer support:

Maintain open communication: Stay available to address questions and offer support as needed.

Monitor progress without micromanaging: Track the task's progress while respecting the team's autonomy.

Offer constructive feedback: Provide regular feedback, acknowledging efforts and suggesting improvements.

Recognize and celebrate results:

Acknowledge good work: Publicly recognize the accomplishments of your team, expressing gratitude and appreciation.

Celebrate successes: Celebrate team achievements, reinforcing collaboration and motivating future efforts.

Create a trust-filled environment: Foster a workplace where individuals feel comfortable taking risks, learning from mistakes, and growing professionally.

Step-by-Step Guide to Applying the "Delegate Tasks" Principle:

Identify tasks: Analyze, prioritize, and identify which activities can be delegated.

Choose people: Assess skills, experience, availability, and potential for growth.

Provide instructions: Explain the objectives, set expectations, and supply resources.

Track progress: Maintain open communication, monitor without micromanaging, and provide feedback.

Recognize results: Celebrate successes, acknowledge efforts, and build trust.

Adjustments if Desired Results Are Not Achieved:

If tasks are not completed successfully: Review the instructions, provide additional support, and adjust expectations.

If resistance to delegation occurs: Explain the benefits of delegation, show trust in your team, and offer development opportunities.

If you feel insecure about delegating: Start with simpler tasks and gradually increase complexity as your confidence grows.

Examples:

A manager delegating meeting organization to an assistant: Provides necessary information, sets a deadline, and trusts their ability to organize the event successfully.

A project leader assigning specific tasks to team members: Utilizes individual skills and experiences to optimize project performance.

A teacher delegating topic research to students: Encourages active learning and student autonomy development.

Delegating tasks is more than lightening your workload; it is a strategy for building stronger teams, fostering collective growth, and achieving objectives more efficiently. Each act of delegation, when executed with purpose and clarity, strengthens your leadership and inspires trust among team members.

By identifying the right tasks, selecting the right people, and providing necessary support, you create a virtuous cycle of productivity and motivation. More than just a technique, delegation is an act of empowerment that demonstrates respect for your team's abilities and potential. Recognizing and celebrating the successes from delegation reinforces collaboration and fosters ongoing commitment.

Effective delegation transforms not only the work process but also your relationship with it. By freeing time for strategic focus, you broaden your vision and enhance your leadership capacity. Apply this principle confidently, and witness how it elevates both your results and the impact you have on those you lead.

Law 22
Cultivate Creativity

Creativity is a transformative force capable of unlocking limitless possibilities and innovative solutions. In a world where change and challenges are constant, cultivating creativity is essential for thriving in both personal and professional life. This skill goes beyond art or technological innovation; it permeates every area of life, enabling you to solve problems, adapt to new circumstances, and stand out in a competitive environment.

Being creative means seeing beyond the obvious, challenging established patterns, and connecting seemingly unrelated ideas to create something new and meaningful. This process is not reserved for geniuses or artists but is accessible to anyone willing to explore, experiment, and learn. Cultivating creativity not only expands your intellectual capabilities but also boosts your self-confidence, as every idea developed and implemented reinforces your belief in your potential.

Creativity plays a crucial role in innovation and communication. Whether developing a revolutionary product or presenting an idea captivatingly, creative thinking enables you to make a profound impact. Additionally, creativity makes you more resilient, helping you face uncertainties with flexibility and optimism.

Cultivating creativity is a continuous exercise in curiosity, experimentation, and courage. It requires openness to new experiences, willingness to learn from mistakes, and the ability to turn the unexpected into opportunities. By embracing your creativity, you discover new ways of thinking, acting, and growing.

Personal Benefits:

Problem-solving: Creativity enables you to find innovative solutions to challenges in your personal and professional life, overcoming obstacles more effectively.

Innovation: Creativity drives innovation, fostering the development of new ideas, products, services, and processes.

Adaptability: Creativity makes you more adaptable to change, allowing you to find flexible solutions and adjust to new realities with ease.

Critical thinking: Creativity enhances critical thinking, enabling you to analyze situations from different perspectives and make more informed decisions.

Effective communication: Creativity makes your communication more engaging and persuasive, helping you express ideas in original and impactful ways.

Increased self-confidence: Developing creativity boosts your self-confidence and belief in your ability to create and innovate.

Application Methods:

Free your mind:

Break patterns: Challenge assumptions, question the status quo, and seek new ways of thinking and acting.

Explore different perspectives: View things from various angles, consider divergent opinions, and seek inspiration from unexpected sources.

Cultivate curiosity: Ask questions, explore new topics, and take an interest in the world around you.

Stimulate your imagination:

Practice brainstorming: Collaborate with others to generate ideas without judgment or criticism, letting creativity flow freely.

Use visual thinking techniques: Create mind maps, drawings, and diagrams to organize ideas and explore new connections.

Immerse yourself in sensory experiences: Visit museums, watch movies, listen to music, explore nature, and draw inspiration from diverse forms of artistic expression.

Experiment and learn from your mistakes:

Don't fear failure: Mistakes are part of the creative process. View them as opportunities for learning and improvement.

Test new ideas: Go beyond thinking about new ideas by putting them into action and trying different approaches.

Seek feedback: Ask for feedback from others about your ideas and solutions, and be open to constructive criticism.

Create an environment conducive to creativity:

Set aside time for creativity: Incorporate creativity into your routine by dedicating time to think, reflect, and explore new ideas.

Surround yourself with creative people: Connect with individuals who inspire your creativity and challenge you to think outside the box.

Design an inspiring space: Organize your workspace to stimulate creativity with colors, images, objects, and elements that spark your imagination.

Step-by-Step Guide to Applying the "Cultivate Creativity" Principle:

Free your mind: Break patterns, explore different perspectives, and cultivate curiosity.

Stimulate your imagination: Brainstorm, use visual thinking techniques, and immerse yourself in sensory experiences.

Experiment and learn: Don't fear failure, test new ideas, and seek feedback.

Create a conducive environment: Set aside time for creativity, surround yourself with creative people, and design an inspiring space.

Adjustments if Desired Results Are Not Achieved:

If you feel stuck in a creative block: Change your routine, try new activities, and seek inspiration from unusual sources.

If your ideas seem too conventional: Challenge assumptions, question the obvious, and seek more original perspectives.

If you struggle to implement your ideas: Break projects into smaller steps, set realistic deadlines, and seek support from others.

Examples:

A writer seeking inspiration for their next book: Travels to unfamiliar places, engages with people from different cultures, and experiments with new forms of artistic expression.

An entrepreneur developing a new product: Conducts brainstorming sessions with their team, analyzes market needs, and draws inspiration from solutions in other industries.

A teacher exploring new teaching methods: Tries different methodologies, uses technological resources, and encourages active student participation.

Cultivating creativity is a commitment to yourself and your transformative potential. By freeing your mind, stimulating your imagination, and creating an environment conducive to creative thinking, you position yourself for success, ready to face challenges with innovative and impactful solutions.

Creativity is not an innate talent but a skill developed through practice and intention. By embracing mistakes, exploring new ideas, and seeking inspiration from diverse sources, you pave the way for surprising discoveries. Surrounding yourself with creative individuals and setting aside time to think and imagine strengthens this process, making it a natural part of your routine.

Remember, creativity is not just a tool for problem-solving or innovation but also a way to enrich your life, broaden your horizons, and turn ideas into reality. Embrace your creative capacity and discover how it can be the key to a more dynamic, adaptable, and fulfilling life.

Law 23
Master Technology

Mastering technology is an essential skill in a world where digital tools shape every aspect of modern life. From increasing productivity at work to expanding learning opportunities, technology is a powerful resource that can transform how you live, connect, and innovate. However, to fully reap its benefits, you must go beyond basic use and learn to apply it strategically.

With the constant advancement of digital tools, technology has become an indispensable ally for solving problems, accessing information, and communicating with people worldwide. By mastering the right tools, you not only optimize your time but also expand your capacity for innovation and collaboration. Moreover, conscious use of technology enhances creativity, allowing you to explore new forms of expression and personal development.

Mastery of technology goes beyond merely using it. It involves developing essential digital skills such as information management and online security and applying them strategically to achieve your goals. Staying updated on technological trends and being willing to adapt to constant changes is also crucial, ensuring you remain ahead in a competitive digital environment.

With an intentional and practical approach, technology becomes a tool that enhances your personal and professional growth. More than a technical resource, it amplifies your vision, connects you to the world, and helps you achieve new levels of efficiency and innovation.

Personal Benefits:

Increased productivity: Digital tools such as organization apps, automation software, and communication platforms allow you to do more in less time.

Expanded opportunities: Technology opens doors to new work, education, business, and networking opportunities with people worldwide.

Improved communication: Online communication platforms facilitate connections with people from different places, cultures, and languages, expanding your networks and collaboration possibilities.

Access to information: The internet provides unlimited access to information, helping you stay updated, learn new subjects, and acquire skills.

Personal growth: Technology offers tools for personal development, including meditation apps, online learning platforms, and habit-tracking tools.

Creativity and innovation: Technology fosters creativity and innovation through tools for content creation, design, music, video, and other forms of artistic expression.

Application Methods:

Choose the right tools:

Define your needs: Identify your goals and needs regarding technology. What tools can help you be more productive, connect with others, or learn new things?

Research and experiment: Explore various apps, software, and online platforms, testing their functionality and evaluating their relevance to your needs.

Invest in quality tools: Prioritize reliable, secure tools that provide adequate technical support.

Develop essential digital skills:

Digital literacy: Master basic computer and internet skills, such as navigation, research, document creation, and online communication.

Information management: Learn to organize, store, and share information securely and efficiently using cloud services, note-taking apps, and file management tools.

Online security: Protect your privacy and personal data online by using strong passwords, antivirus software, and safe browsing habits.

Use technology strategically:

Task automation: Use automation tools to streamline repetitive tasks such as scheduling posts, sending emails, and paying bills.

Time management: Use calendar apps, task lists, and time management tools to organize your routine and boost productivity.

Online learning: Take advantage of online platforms to acquire new knowledge and skills through courses, tutorials, and video lessons.

Stay updated:

Follow the trends: Stay informed about new technologies, trends, and digital tools by reading blogs, specialized websites, and attending events and courses.

Adapt to change: Be open to learning and adapting to constant changes in the tech world by cultivating a flexible and innovative mindset.

Share your knowledge: Help others benefit from digital tools by sharing your expertise and guiding them in navigating the digital world.

Step-by-Step Guide to Applying the "Master Technology" Principle:

Select tools: Define your needs, research options, and experiment with different tools.

Develop skills: Master digital literacy, information management, and online security.

Use strategically: Automate tasks, manage time effectively, and embrace online learning.

Stay updated: Follow trends, adapt to changes, and share your knowledge with others.

Adjustments if Desired Results Are Not Achieved:

If you feel overwhelmed by technology: Simplify your tools, disable unnecessary notifications, and set limits for digital device use.

If you struggle to learn new tools: Seek tutorials, online courses, or support from more experienced individuals.

If you're concerned about online privacy: Review privacy settings on your accounts, use strong passwords, and adopt safe browsing practices.

Examples:

A professional using project management tools: Organizes tasks and collaborates with the team online to streamline workflows.

A student utilizing online learning platforms: Complements studies and connects with students worldwide to share knowledge.

An artist using image and video editing software: Creates original content and shares it on social media to engage audiences.

Mastering technology unlocks a universe of possibilities, from increased productivity to expanded creativity and opportunities. Using digital tools with purpose and strategy transforms how you live and work, paving the way for a more efficient and connected life.

Remember, true mastery of technology is not just about keeping up with trends but integrating them intelligently into your routine. Whether automating tasks, learning new skills, or connecting with people globally, every step in this direction brings you closer to your goals and amplifies your impact.

Adopting a mindset of continuous learning and openness to technological innovation ensures you not only keep pace with change but also lead transformations. By sharing your knowledge and helping others navigate the digital world, you multiply technology's benefits and strengthen your own journey. Make technology your ally and discover how it can take you further than you ever imagined.

Law 24
Invest in Learning

Investing in learning is one of the most powerful decisions you can make to transform your life. In a world where change is the only constant, continuous learning empowers you to adapt, grow, and thrive amidst new challenges and opportunities. More than an academic or professional activity, learning is a vital process that broadens horizons, develops skills, and enriches your understanding of the world.

Adopting a growth mindset is the first step to unlocking the power of learning. Viewing challenges as opportunities and believing in your ability to evolve are attitudes that pave the way to success. Whether through formal education, self-directed methods, or exchanging experiences with mentors and peers, learning opportunities are unlimited and accessible to all.

Learning transcends knowledge acquisition—it becomes truly transformative when applied in practice, whether solving problems, experimenting with new approaches, or sharing insights with others. This cycle of learning, application, and reflection solidifies knowledge and turns it into competence.

Investing in learning not only propels your career forward but also enriches your life overall. It boosts your self-confidence, enhances decision-making skills, and provides a continuous sense of accomplishment. Whatever your interests or goals, learning is the key to unlocking your true potential and reaching new heights.

Personal Benefits:

Adaptability: Continuous learning enables you to adapt to changes in the job market, new technologies, and the demands of an evolving world.

Professional growth: Investing in learning opens doors to new opportunities, promotions, and increased income.

Increased self-confidence: Acquiring new knowledge and skills strengthens your confidence in overcoming challenges and achieving your goals.

Better decision-making: Knowledge expands your perspective, improves analytical skills, and supports more informed and effective decisions.

Mental stimulation: Lifelong learning keeps your mind active, sharp, and creative, preventing cognitive decline and promoting mental health.

Personal fulfillment: The pursuit of knowledge and skill development brings a sense of purpose, accomplishment, and individual growth.

Application Methods:

Cultivate a growth mindset:

Embrace challenges: See challenges as opportunities to learn and grow rather than obstacles to avoid.

Believe in your potential: Trust in your ability to learn and develop, regardless of age or prior experience.

Value effort: Recognize that learning requires effort and dedication, and celebrate your achievements along the way.

Identify learning opportunities:

Formal education: Consider degree programs, certifications, or courses to deepen knowledge in areas of interest.

Informal learning: Explore books, articles, blogs, online lectures, workshops, and conferences for accessible learning options.

Mentorship and networking: Seek guidance from experienced mentors and participate in networking events to learn from others and share experiences.

Master different learning methods:

Active learning: Engage in the learning process by asking questions, participating in discussions, doing exercises, and applying knowledge in practice.

Visual learning: Use visual aids like charts, diagrams, and videos to better understand and retain information.

Auditory learning: Listen to lectures, podcasts, and audiobooks to absorb information through auditory means.

Apply knowledge in practice:

Experimentation: Apply what you've learned in real-life situations by testing your skills and using your knowledge in projects or daily challenges.

Reflection: Reflect on your learning experiences to identify strengths and weaknesses and seek ways to improve your skills.

Sharing: Share your knowledge with others by teaching, mentoring, or participating in group discussions.

Step-by-Step Guide to Applying the "Invest in Learning" Principle:

Cultivate a growth mindset: Embrace challenges, believe in your potential, and value effort.

Identify opportunities: Explore formal education, informal learning, mentorship, and networking.

Master methods: Experiment with active, visual, and auditory learning to find what works best for you.

Apply knowledge: Experiment, reflect, and share your insights with others.

Adjustments if Desired Results Are Not Achieved:

If you struggle to stay motivated: Set clear and specific learning goals, find a study partner, or seek a mentor to support you on your journey.

If you feel overwhelmed by information: Prioritize topics of interest, organize study time, and use knowledge management tools.

If you find it hard to apply knowledge: Look for opportunities to practice skills, such as volunteering, personal projects, or joining competitions.

Examples:

A professional pursuing a specialization course: Updates their knowledge in their field to enhance promotion prospects.

An entrepreneur reading business management books: Improves decision-making and hones leadership skills.

An artist attending workshops: Learns new techniques and develops their unique style.

Investing in learning is a continuous and rewarding journey that extends far beyond simply accumulating knowledge. It's a path to personal growth, broader perspectives, and tackling challenges with greater confidence and preparation. By adopting a growth mindset, identifying opportunities, and applying your learning in practice, you not only enhance your skills but also inspire positive changes in your life and those around you.

Remember, learning is not a destination but a lifelong process. Even when results aren't immediate, every effort contributes to consistent and meaningful progress. Explore different ways of learning, whether through books, courses, mentors, or hands-on experiences, and discover the method that best suits your style and goals.

By sharing your knowledge and reflecting on your achievements, you multiply the impact of learning, creating a virtuous cycle of growth and fulfillment. Invest in yourself, keep learning, and reap the rewards of a life full of possibilities and accomplishments.

Law 25
Promote Diversity

Promoting diversity is one of the pillars for building richer, fairer, and more innovative environments. In a world where differences are often seen as barriers, it's essential to recognize them as invaluable sources of strength and growth. Diversity not only broadens perspectives but also inspires empathy, creativity, and collaboration, making individuals and communities more resilient and prepared to face future challenges.

Embracing diversity requires a mindset shift, starting with identifying and dismantling both conscious and unconscious biases. This paves the way for creating inclusive environments where differences are respected, and people feel valued for their uniqueness. Beyond being an ethical initiative, diversity is a strategic advantage that drives success in workplaces, organizations, and social interactions.

Diversity fuels creativity and innovation, introducing new ideas and approaches to solving problems and achieving goals. When different perspectives converge, more effective and transformative solutions emerge. Simultaneously, diversity strengthens interpersonal bonds and fosters a more just society where everyone has the opportunity to contribute and thrive.

Promoting diversity is a shared responsibility that begins with individual attitudes and expands to collective actions. Through knowledge, effort, and commitment, it's possible to transform prejudice into understanding and exclusion into inclusion, creating a world where differences are celebrated as common wealth.

Personal Benefits:

Broadened perspectives: Diversity enriches your worldview by exposing you to different viewpoints, ideas, and experiences, resulting in a more comprehensive and nuanced understanding.

Personal development: Interacting with people from diverse backgrounds and cultures fosters personal growth, empathy, and mutual understanding.

Creativity and innovation: Diversity drives creativity and innovation by bringing unique perspectives and approaches to problem-solving and solution creation.

Strengthened relationships: Promoting diversity and inclusion builds stronger interpersonal relationships founded on trust and mutual respect.

A more equitable society: Supporting diversity contributes to building a fairer, more equitable, and welcoming society for all.

Increased social awareness: Understanding the importance of diversity enhances your social awareness and commitment to combating discrimination and injustice.

Application Methods:

Combat prejudice:

Identify your own biases: Recognize and challenge your unconscious biases and prejudices through education, reflection, and interaction with people from different backgrounds.

Question stereotypes: Challenge stereotypes and generalizations about groups of people by seeking to know individuals and their unique stories and experiences.

Advocate for equality: Speak out against discrimination and prejudice, and support equal opportunities for all, regardless of their background or identity.

Create an inclusive environment:

Promote respect and appreciation for differences: Foster an atmosphere where everyone feels respected, valued, and safe to express their authentic selves.

Encourage active participation: Ensure everyone has the opportunity to contribute their ideas and perspectives.

Provide equal opportunities: Guarantee that all individuals have access to the same opportunities, regardless of their background or identity.

Leverage the benefits of diversity:

Build diverse teams: Assemble teams with people from varied backgrounds, skills, and perspectives to capitalize on the benefits of diverse thought and experience.

Seek different viewpoints: Encourage dialogue and idea-sharing among individuals with different perspectives to enrich discussions and find creative and innovative solutions.

Value contributions: Recognize and celebrate the contributions of each team member, highlighting the richness that diversity brings to the workplace.

Be a change agent:

Educate yourself on diversity and inclusion: Seek knowledge and information about diversity, inclusion, and social justice to better understand the challenges and opportunities associated with these issues.

Share your knowledge: Spread awareness about the importance of diversity and inclusion by sharing what you've learned with others.

Drive change in your community: Initiate actions and initiatives that promote diversity and inclusion in your community, such as events, talks, and awareness campaigns.

Step-by-Step Guide to Applying the "Promote Diversity" Principle:

Combat prejudice: Identify biases, challenge stereotypes, and advocate for equality.

Create an inclusive environment: Promote respect, encourage participation, and ensure equal opportunities.

Leverage benefits: Build diverse teams, seek different perspectives, and value individual contributions.

Be a change agent: Educate yourself, share knowledge, and drive change in your community.

Adjustments if Desired Results Are Not Achieved:

If resistance to diversity arises: Engage in open dialogue about diversity's benefits, present data and concrete examples, and seek support from leaders and influencers who share your values.

If you identify shortcomings in your own practices: Be open to learning from your mistakes, seek feedback from diverse individuals, and adjust your actions to foster a more inclusive culture.

If you feel discouraged by challenges: Remember that promoting diversity is a continuous journey requiring persistence and commitment. Connect with like-minded individuals and celebrate small victories along the way.

Examples:

A company implementing diversity-focused hiring programs: Attracts talent from underrepresented groups to build a more inclusive workforce.

A school organizing activities and discussions on different cultures and identities: Fosters an inclusive environment and combats prejudice among students.

A community leader hosting events to promote gender equality and women's empowerment: Raises awareness and encourages participation in building a more equitable society.

Promoting diversity benefits not only those around you but also yourself. By creating space for varied perspectives and experiences, you enrich your worldview, strengthen your relationships, and contribute to building a fairer, more inclusive society.

Remember, diversity is not just an ethical value but also a powerful tool for personal and collective growth. Whether assembling diverse teams, fostering inclusive environments, or challenging prejudices, every action helps transform realities and inspire positive change.

Though the path to inclusion may present challenges, it offers significant rewards. By educating yourself about diversity and sharing your learnings, you become a change agent capable of leading by example and encouraging others to follow suit. With persistence and empathy, you can help create a future where diversity is celebrated as an essential force for progress and harmony.

Law 26
Practice Resilience

Practicing resilience is a fundamental skill for overcoming adversity and thriving, even in the face of life's toughest challenges. Resilience doesn't just mean enduring difficult moments—it's about transforming them into opportunities for learning, growth, and personal strength. In a world full of uncertainties, resilience enables you to rise after a fall and move forward, wiser and more confident than before.

Resilience begins with a positive mindset that focuses on solutions and opportunities rather than problems. This perspective allows you to see difficulties as temporary and surmountable. It's strengthened by self-awareness, self-care, and building a robust support network of friends, family, and professionals who can offer emotional guidance.

Beyond emotional fortitude, resilience is also a daily practice. It involves analyzing situations with clarity, learning from mistakes, and reframing negative experiences to extract valuable lessons. Resilience is an active process requiring effort and dedication but yielding significant rewards: better mental health, stronger relationships, and unwavering self-confidence.

Cultivating resilience isn't just about surviving—it's about thriving. By practicing resilience, you tap into an inner strength that helps you weather life's storms with courage, adapt to change, and emerge stronger than ever.

Personal Benefits:

Overcoming challenges: Resilience equips you to face and overcome life's obstacles with greater courage and determination, including losses, failures, illnesses, or crises.

Personal growth: Adversity and mistakes become opportunities for learning and growth, making you stronger and wiser.

Adaptability: Resilience enhances your ability to adapt to changes and find creative solutions to emerging problems.

Mental health and well-being: Resilient individuals enjoy better mental health and emotional well-being, effectively managing stress, anxiety, and depression.

Stronger relationships: Resilience fosters deeper, more supportive relationships by enabling you to give and receive help during tough times.

Increased self-confidence: Overcoming adversity builds self-confidence and trust in your ability to handle any situation.

Application Methods:

Cultivate a positive mindset:

Focus on solutions: Shift your attention from problems to solutions and possibilities.

Practice gratitude: Appreciate the good things in your life, even during difficult times.

Maintain optimism: Believe in your ability to overcome challenges and that better days are ahead.

Develop inner strength:

Self-awareness: Connect with yourself, understand your strengths and weaknesses, and identify your values and life purpose.

Self-care: Prioritize your physical and mental health through exercise, proper nutrition, sufficient sleep, and leisure activities.

Spirituality: Find strength and meaning through spirituality, whether via religion, meditation, or connecting with nature.

Build a support network:

Strengthen relationships: Cultivate positive relationships with friends, family, and trusted individuals who can provide support during tough times.

Seek professional help: Don't hesitate to consult therapists or counselors if facing emotional or psychological difficulties.

Join support groups: Connect with people who've faced similar experiences to share stories and offer mutual support.

Learn from mistakes and adversity:

Analyze the situation: Reflect on negative experiences objectively, identifying contributing factors and lessons to be learned.

Reframe the experience: View negative experiences from a new perspective, finding positive aspects and growth opportunities.

Move forward: Don't let fear or guilt hold you back. Forgive yourself, accept what happened, and proceed with greater strength and wisdom.

Step-by-Step Guide to Applying the "Practice Resilience" Principle:

Cultivate a positive mindset: Focus on solutions, practice gratitude, and maintain optimism.

Develop inner strength: Invest in self-awareness, self-care, and spirituality.

Build a support network: Strengthen relationships and seek help when needed.

Learn from mistakes: Analyze, reframe, and move forward with renewed purpose.

Adjustments if Desired Results Are Not Achieved:

If recovering from trauma feels difficult: Seek professional help from a psychologist or psychiatrist to process emotions and develop coping mechanisms.

If you feel demotivated or drained: Revisit your life goals, seek new sources of inspiration, and make small changes to your routine to regain enthusiasm.

If repeating the same mistakes: Reflect on behavior patterns, identify triggers, and develop strategies to avoid them in the future.

Examples:

An athlete recovering from a serious injury: Returns to competing at a high level by focusing on rehabilitation and mental strength.

An entrepreneur rebuilding after business failure: Learns from past mistakes and creates a successful new enterprise.

A person coping with the loss of a loved one: Finds the strength to honor their memory and continue celebrating life.

Practicing resilience is a journey of self-discovery and personal growth that transforms challenges into opportunities. It doesn't eliminate adversity but changes how you face it, enabling you to overcome each obstacle with courage, clarity, and determination.

By cultivating a positive mindset, investing in inner strength, and seeking support when needed, you build a strong foundation for navigating life's highs and lows. Every challenge overcome reinforces your self-confidence and reminds you of your capacity to handle any situation.

Practicing resilience doesn't mean avoiding mistakes but learning from them. Reframing negative experiences and moving forward with purpose allows you to grow and thrive even during tough times. Remember, resilience is like a muscle that strengthens with use, and every challenge faced is an opportunity to make it more robust. Embrace resilience as a guiding principle and discover the extraordinary strength within you.

Law 27
Communicate Effectively

Effective communication is an essential skill for success in all aspects of life. Whether strengthening personal relationships or achieving professional goals, the way you convey your ideas and interpret others' messages plays a crucial role. Effective communication ensures your message is understood, fosters deeper connections, promotes collaboration, and facilitates conflict resolution.

Good communication starts with clarity. Organizing your thoughts, using accessible language, and structuring your message logically are indispensable steps to ensuring it is understood without ambiguity. But effective communication goes beyond words: smart use of body language, tone of voice, and tools like storytelling make your messages more engaging and memorable.

Being a good listener is just as important as expressing yourself well. Attentive listening, showing genuine interest, and responding constructively strengthen trust and empathy in interactions. This approach not only helps avoid misunderstandings but also enriches relationships and fosters an environment of respect and collaboration.

The art of effective communication is a skill that can be developed with practice and dedication. By mastering it, you'll be better prepared to influence, inspire, and achieve your goals while building meaningful connections with those around you.

Personal Benefits:

Clarity and understanding: Effective communication ensures your messages are correctly understood, avoiding misunderstandings and confusion.

Building relationships: Clear and empathetic communication strengthens interpersonal relationships, creating deeper and more meaningful connections.

Influence and persuasion: Effective communication enhances your ability to influence and persuade, enabling you to inspire others, motivate actions, and achieve goals more easily.

Conflict resolution: It helps prevent and resolve conflicts constructively by expressing your needs and understanding others' perspectives.

Increased productivity: Clear and objective communication in the workplace improves productivity by avoiding time lost to misunderstandings.

Personal and professional development: Mastering communication is a valuable skill that opens doors to personal and professional growth.

Application Methods:

Express your ideas clearly:

Organize your thoughts: Before speaking or writing, organize your thoughts and define the core message you want to convey.

Use clear and concise language: Avoid jargon, technical terms, and complex sentences that might confuse your audience. Choose simple and direct words.

Structure your message: Break your message into clear topics and use visual aids like charts and images to make it easier to understand.

Build engaging narratives:

Use storytelling: Stories captivate your audience's attention, convey emotions, and make your message more memorable.

Create relatable characters: Introduce characters your audience can identify with, creating an emotional connection to your message.

Present a conflict and resolution: Craft a narrative with a conflict that creates tension and a resolution that satisfies your audience.

Use body language effectively:

Maintain eye contact: Look into your listener's eyes to show confidence and interest.

Use expressive gestures: Complement your words with gestures to make your communication more dynamic and engaging.

Adopt an open posture: Avoid crossing your arms or leaning back, as this may convey disinterest or defensiveness.

Master different communication channels:

Verbal communication: Practice public speaking skills, focusing on tone of voice, speech pace, and body language.

Written communication: Hone your writing skills to be clear, concise, and grammatically accurate.

Online communication: Learn to use digital tools like email, instant messaging, and video conferencing effectively, tailoring your language and style to each platform.

Be a good listener:

Pay attention: Focus on what the other person is saying without distractions or interruptions.

Show interest: Ask questions, nod, and use facial expressions to demonstrate engagement.

Paraphrase: Repeat what the other person said in your own words to ensure understanding.

Step-by-Step Guide to Applying the "Communicate Effectively" Principle:

Define your objective: What message do you want to convey, and what outcome do you hope to achieve?

Know your audience: Who is your target audience? What are their interests, needs, and expectations?

Prepare your message: Organize your thoughts, use clear and concise language, and structure your message logically.

Choose the right communication channel: Decide whether verbal, written, or online communication is best for your message.

Communicate with confidence: Speak clearly, use body language effectively, and listen attentively.

Adjustments if Desired Results Are Not Achieved:

If your message isn't understood: Simplify your language, use examples and analogies, and ask for feedback from your audience.

If you fail to connect with your audience: Adapt your communication style to suit their preferences and demonstrate empathy and genuine interest.

If you don't achieve the desired response: Revise your message, adjust your approach, and experiment with different communication channels.

Examples:

A leader inspiring their team: Delivers a motivational speech using clear language, impactful visuals, and an inspiring story.

A negotiator closing an important deal: Communicates clearly, concisely, and persuasively while listening attentively to the other party's needs.

A teacher explaining a complex concept: Simplifies the idea with practical examples, visual aids, and accessible language.

Practicing effective communication transforms your interactions, amplifies your influence, and enriches your relationships. By expressing yourself clearly, employing strategies like storytelling, and using body language effectively, you make your messages more impactful and engaging.

Remember, effective communication is not just about transmitting information but also about creating mutual understanding and emotional connection. Active listening and demonstrating empathy are fundamental pillars for building trust and cooperation in communication.

Whether in personal or professional contexts, effective communication bridges the gap between your ideas and the people you engage with. Mastering this skill opens doors to opportunities, resolves conflicts gracefully, and strengthens your position as a trustworthy and influential leader. Practice, refine, and value your communication, and enjoy the rewards of a world that understands and appreciates your message.

Law 28
Use Language Effectively

Language is one of humanity's most powerful tools. It enables us not only to convey information but also to build connections, inspire action, and turn ideas into reality. When used effectively, language can influence, persuade, and create a lasting impact on people and the world around you. Mastering this skill is essential for achieving personal and professional success.

Communication extends far beyond words. Tone of voice, body language, and even visual symbols play a crucial role in how your messages are received and interpreted. Using these nuances consciously and strategically is what distinguishes an ordinary communicator from an exceptional one.

Moreover, language is a reflection of thought. Expanding your vocabulary, mastering grammar, and structuring your ideas clearly and engagingly enhance not only how you communicate but also how you think. The ability to adapt your language to your audience, context, and communication objectives is a valuable skill that increases your influence and effectiveness in any situation.

The conscious practice of language is an opportunity for self-discovery, empowerment, and transformation. When you master words—spoken, written, or visual—you build bridges that connect ideas to people and people to change.

Personal Benefits:

Effective communication: Mastering language allows you to communicate clearly, concisely, and persuasively, ensuring your messages resonate and are easily understood.

Relationship building: Language is the foundation of human connection. Using it with empathy and authenticity strengthens relationships and deepens bonds.

Influence and persuasion: Language is a powerful tool for influence. Strategically employing words, tone, and body language enhances your persuasive abilities and leadership.

Personal expression: Language enables you to authentically and creatively express your thoughts, emotions, and ideas.

Professional growth: Proficiency in language is essential for career success, from communicating with colleagues and clients to presenting projects and ideas.

Self-awareness: Language reflects your thoughts. Analyzing how you communicate can lead to greater self-awareness and understanding.

Application Methods:

Master verbal language:

Expand your vocabulary: Learn new words and expressions to articulate your thoughts with greater precision and richness.

Improve grammar and syntax: Master grammatical rules and sentence structure to communicate clearly and correctly.

Control tone of voice: Adjust your tone to suit the situation and message, using emphasis, pauses, and intonation to create impact and convey emotion.

Master nonverbal language:

Body language: Be mindful of posture, gestures, facial expressions, and eye contact, using them intentionally to reinforce your messages and create presence.

Proxemics: Use physical space strategically, adjusting proximity to your audience based on the level of intimacy and nature of the interaction.

Paralinguistics: Pay attention to vocal cues beyond speech, such as laughter, sighs, and approval or disapproval sounds, as they convey important emotional and reactive information.

Harness the power of symbolic language:

Metaphors and analogies: Use these tools to make your messages more vivid, memorable, and persuasive, creating impactful mental associations.

Storytelling: Tell stories to communicate complex ideas in an engaging and memorable way, forming emotional connections with your audience.

Visual symbols: Leverage images, colors, logos, and other visual symbols to reinforce your messages and build a strong and cohesive identity.

Adapt your language to the context:

Know your audience: Tailor your language to your audience, considering their age, knowledge level, culture, and interests.

Clarify your objective: Adjust your language to align with your communication goal, whether to inform, persuade, entertain, or inspire.

Consider the environment: Adapt your language to suit the setting, whether it's a formal meeting, casual conversation, or public presentation.

Step-by-Step Guide to Applying the "Use Language Effectively" Principle:

Master the basics: Enhance your vocabulary, grammar, and syntax.

Practice nonverbal communication: Focus on body language, proxemics, and paralinguistics.

Explore symbolic language: Use metaphors, analogies, and storytelling.

Adapt your language: Align your communication to the audience, objective, and environment.

Adjustments if Desired Results Are Not Achieved:

If your message isn't understood: Simplify your language, provide examples, and ask for feedback from your audience.

If you fail to connect with your audience: Adapt your language and style to their preferences and demonstrate empathy and understanding.

If you don't get the desired response: Review your message, refine your approach, and experiment with different ways of expressing yourself.

Examples:

A politician inspiring voters: Uses emotive language and impactful imagery to persuade the electorate.

A religious leader teaching spiritual lessons: Employs parables and metaphors to make teachings relatable and meaningful.

An advertiser creating a campaign: Combines creative language and striking visuals to capture attention and drive engagement.

Using language effectively is an art that can be learned, practiced, and refined throughout life. Mastering not just what you say but how you say it transforms you into an impactful communicator capable of inspiring, persuading, and building strong relationships.

When verbal and nonverbal language are combined strategically, they create richer and more engaging messages. Exploring the power of metaphors, storytelling, and visual symbols transforms ideas into memorable experiences that captivate and influence your audience.

Remember, the key to effective communication lies in adaptation. Adjusting your message to the context and understanding your audience's preferences ensures your language achieves the desired outcome. By investing in this skill, you're investing in yourself, expanding your possibilities for connection, growth, and success. Practice, experiment, and discover the transformative power of language.

Law 29
Captivate Audiences

Captivating an audience is an essential skill for those who wish to influence, inspire, and leave a lasting impression. Whether in a meeting room, on stage, or at a social gathering, the ability to grab and hold attention while creating genuine connections can turn your messages into memorable experiences. Captivation goes beyond simply sharing information—it's about engaging, evoking emotion, and motivating people to think or act differently.

The foundation of captivating an audience is connection. Understanding your audience, addressing their expectations, and using stories, humor, and empathy are crucial strategies for building an emotional bond. This connection is reinforced by a confident stage presence, where body language, tone of voice, and enthusiasm work in harmony to maintain interest.

Visual and audiovisual resources also play a key role, illustrating concepts and enhancing your presentation. However, they should be used strategically to complement, not overshadow, your core message. Additionally, adapting your language, tone, and content to the context and audience profile ensures your message resonates more profoundly.

Captivating an audience is more than a technique—it's a way to express authenticity and passion while sharing your ideas engagingly and impactfully. With practice and intention, this skill becomes a powerful tool to transform interactions and achieve your goals.

Personal Benefits:

Influence and persuasion: Captivating an audience enhances your ability to communicate ideas with greater impact and persuasion.

Relationship building: Establishing genuine connections with your audience strengthens relationships and opens doors to new collaboration opportunities.

Increased self-confidence: Mastering the art of captivating audiences boosts self-confidence and your ability to communicate clearly and assertively.

Improved professional performance: In presentations, meetings, or negotiations, captivating an audience enhances your professional effectiveness and success.

Leadership skills development: The ability to captivate audiences is a hallmark of inspiring leaders who motivate and rally others around a shared vision.

Creative expression: Captivating audiences allows you to showcase your creativity and present ideas in original and engaging ways.

Application Methods:

Connect with your audience:

Know your audience: Research your audience's interests, needs, and expectations before any presentation.

Establish eye contact: Make direct eye contact to create an individual connection and demonstrate confidence and interest.

Share personal stories: Personal anecdotes foster empathy and connection, making your message more relatable and memorable.

Use humor: Humor is a powerful tool for breaking the ice, lightening the atmosphere, and making your presentation more enjoyable.

Build a magnetic stage presence:

Body language: Use confident and expressive body language, such as open gestures, upright posture, and natural movements.

Voice: Project your voice clearly and convincingly, varying tone, pace, and intonation to keep the audience engaged.

Enthusiasm: Show passion and enthusiasm for your topic, energizing the audience with your positivity and commitment.

Use audiovisual resources effectively:

Impactful visuals: Use high-quality images that complement your message and create visual impact.

Engaging videos: Short and compelling videos can illustrate concepts, tell stories, and maintain audience interest.

Concise, organized slides: Design clear, concise, and well-organized presentations, avoiding excessive text or clutter.

Adapt your message to your audience:

Context: Tailor your message to the presentation's setting, whether it's a business meeting, academic lecture, or social event.

Language: Use language appropriate to the audience's knowledge level and interests.

Tone: Adjust your tone to match the event's formality and audience expectations.

Step-by-Step Guide to Applying the "Captivate Audiences" Principle:

Know your audience: Research their interests, needs, and expectations.

Prepare your message: Define your presentation's purpose and structure your content clearly and engagingly.

Practice your stage presence: Hone your body language, voice, and facial expressions.

Use audiovisual aids: Select impactful visuals, videos, and slides that enhance your message.

Adapt your message: Tailor your language, tone, and content to fit the context and audience.

Adjustments if Desired Results Are Not Achieved:

If the audience seems disengaged: Vary your tone of voice, ask questions, share stories, or use more stimulating visuals.

If you feel nervous: Take deep breaths, focus on your message, and remember the audience wants you to succeed.

If you fail to connect with the audience: Seek feedback from trusted sources and adjust your approach to create a more genuine connection.

Examples:

A teacher: Uses visual aids and engaging stories to keep students attentive and interested during lessons.

A motivational speaker: Captivates the audience with energy, humor, and personal anecdotes, inspiring and motivating listeners.

A musician: Connects emotionally with the audience through music, creating an atmosphere of shared experience and emotion.

Captivating audiences is an art that combines preparation, presence, and passion. By understanding your audience, tailoring your message, and skillfully employing visual and emotional resources, you create presentations that leave a lasting impact.

Remember, connection is the heart of every successful interaction. Sharing authentic stories, demonstrating empathy, and conveying enthusiasm strengthen this bond, turning a passive audience into engaged participants.

Even when faced with challenges like nervousness or initial disinterest, consistent practice and adaptability refine your approach, allowing you to reach new levels of effectiveness. Captivating an audience is not just about delivering ideas—it's about creating meaningful moments that inspire, transform, and unite people around a common purpose. Be confident, authentic, and bold, and discover the power of truly connecting with those who listen to you.

Law 30
Present Ideas

Presenting ideas effectively is an essential skill for turning thoughts into actions, inspiring change, and achieving goals. Whether in corporate, academic, or social settings, the ability to convey your ideas with clarity, impact, and passion can open doors, strengthen relationships, and elevate your influence.

An effective presentation goes beyond sharing information—it's an invitation for the audience to embrace your vision. This begins with a well-structured approach: an attention-grabbing introduction, clear and compelling development, and a conclusion that motivates action or reflection. Strategic use of visual aids, such as images and graphs, reinforces your message, while a confident delivery supported by expressive body language keeps the audience engaged.

Adapting your presentation to the context and audience is equally crucial. Understanding the expectations and interests of your listeners ensures your message resonates deeply. Preparation and practice are key to building confidence and managing unexpected challenges, allowing you to focus on connecting with your audience authentically.

Presenting ideas isn't just a tool for communication—it's a way to create impact. Each successful presentation is an opportunity to showcase your potential, inspire others, and drive meaningful change.

Personal Benefits:

Influence and persuasion: Effective presentations increase your ability to persuade, gain support for projects, and inspire action.

Improved communication skills: Mastering presentations enhances overall communication, making you a clearer, more concise, and impactful communicator.

Professional growth: The ability to present convincingly opens doors to promotions, new opportunities, and recognition.

Boosted self-confidence: Presenting ideas with clarity and poise strengthens self-confidence and belief in your abilities.

Enhanced creativity: Preparing presentations stimulates innovative thinking, encouraging creative solutions and fresh perspectives.

Stronger teamwork: Collaborative idea-sharing fosters consensus-building and strengthens team dynamics.

Application Methods:

Structure your presentation:

Define the objective: Clearly identify what you aim to achieve—inform, persuade, inspire, or entertain.

Organize your ideas: Create a logical, cohesive flow that makes sense to the audience.

Craft a captivating introduction: Start with a hook to grab attention, introducing the topic and its significance.

Develop the content clearly: Present your ideas with clarity, supported by examples, data, and evidence.

End with a call to action: Summarize key points and encourage the audience to act on your ideas.

Use impactful visual aids:

Concise, visually appealing slides: Keep slides simple with minimal text, high-quality images, and clear graphics.

Engaging videos and animations: Use short, relevant videos to illustrate concepts and captivate attention.

Demonstrations or prototypes: When possible, use tangible examples to make ideas more concrete and relatable.

Master the art of oratory:

Speak with clarity and confidence: Project your voice, maintain a steady pace, and articulate your points clearly.

Leverage body language: Use eye contact, expressive gestures, and confident posture to reinforce your delivery.

Connect with the audience: Show enthusiasm for your topic, ask questions, and encourage participation.

Adapt your approach to different contexts and audiences:

Adjust formality: Match the presentation's tone to the setting, whether a business meeting, academic lecture, or casual gathering.

Know your audience: Tailor your language, tone, and content to their knowledge level, age, and interests.

Manage time effectively: Align your presentation length and content with the available time, ensuring a thorough yet concise delivery.

Step-by-Step Guide to Applying the "Present Ideas" Principle:

Define your objective and audience: Understand what you want to achieve and who you are addressing.

Organize your ideas: Create a logical structure with a clear beginning, middle, and end.

Incorporate visual aids: Use impactful visuals and media to support your message.

Practice delivery: Hone your oratory skills and body language for confident presentations.

Tailor to context and audience: Adjust your style and content to suit the environment and listener expectations.

Adjustments if Desired Results Are Not Achieved:

If the audience appears disengaged or confused: Simplify your language, add examples and visual aids, and encourage interaction.

If you feel nervous or insecure: Practice in advance, take deep breaths, and focus on conveying your message with conviction.

If your message fails to persuade: Revisit your arguments, strengthen your evidence, and refine your approach to better align with audience needs.

Examples:

An entrepreneur pitching to investors: Delivers a compelling business plan with market data, a concise pitch, and visually appealing slides.

A scientist sharing research findings: Uses clear language, graphs, and visuals to explain complex results to a lay audience.

An artist presenting their work: Speaks passionately about their creations, supported by impactful imagery that conveys emotion and meaning.

Presenting ideas effectively is a blend of thoughtful planning, creativity, and emotional connection. By structuring your content clearly, leveraging impactful visuals, and delivering with confidence and enthusiasm, your presentations go beyond informing—they captivate and inspire.

Remember, the success of a presentation isn't just in the content but in how it's delivered. Demonstrating empathy for your audience, adapting language to the context, and inviting interaction build a powerful connection between you and your listeners.

With consistent practice and refinement, presenting ideas becomes more than a skill—it's a gateway to influence, innovation, and leadership. Each presentation is an opportunity to leave your mark and take your ideas to new heights. Embrace it as a chance to inspire, engage, and drive meaningful change.

Law 31
Manage Expectations

Managing expectations is a critical skill for fostering harmonious relationships, preventing conflicts, and achieving positive outcomes across various aspects of life. By setting and communicating clear, realistic expectations, you create an environment of trust, collaboration, and mutual understanding—key elements for the success of projects, negotiations, and personal relationships.

Effective expectation management begins with clearly defining goals, roles, and available resources. Communicate what can be achieved and how, ensuring alignment among all parties. Assertive communication combined with active listening helps you understand and adjust individual expectations, fostering respect and empathy.

When faced with unrealistic expectations, the ability to negotiate and redefine objectives becomes essential. This not only minimizes frustration but also reinforces trust and a shared commitment to constructive problem-solving. Celebrating successes and providing regular feedback on progress further strengthens relationships and ensures ongoing alignment.

Managing expectations is not just about organization—it's about building human connections grounded in transparency and trust. This practice nurtures an environment where all parties feel valued and engaged, boosting satisfaction, productivity, and overall well-being.

Personal Benefits:

Conflict reduction: Clear and realistic expectations minimize misunderstandings and conflicts by ensuring all parties are aligned on goals, responsibilities, and expected outcomes.

Trust building: Transparent communication and well-defined expectations foster trust in both personal and professional relationships.

Improved communication: Managing expectations encourages open, honest dialogue, allowing people to express their needs and concerns more clearly.

Increased satisfaction: Setting and meeting realistic expectations enhances satisfaction for everyone involved, whether in a project, relationship, or negotiation.

Productivity boost: In the workplace, managing expectations improves productivity by ensuring teams are aligned on objectives and deadlines.

Stress reduction: Clear expectations reduce stress and anxiety, avoiding frustration and disappointment caused by unrealistic or poorly communicated goals.

Application Methods:

Set clear expectations:

Define objectives and goals: Be specific when setting objectives, using measurable criteria and realistic timelines.

Clarify roles and responsibilities: Clearly define who is responsible for what in a project or relationship.

Communicate available resources: Be transparent about the resources at hand, such as time, budget, or personnel, to avoid unrealistic expectations.

Communicate assertively:

Open and honest communication: Share your expectations clearly, concisely, and respectfully, expressing your needs assertively without being confrontational.

Active listening: Pay close attention to others' expectations, understanding their perspectives and concerns.

Provide regular feedback: Offer ongoing updates on progress and fulfillment of expectations, enabling adjustments as needed.

Handle unrealistic expectations:

Negotiate and be flexible: Be open to renegotiating and redefining expectations when they prove unattainable.

Assertive explanation: Respectfully explain why certain expectations cannot be met, and propose viable alternatives or solutions.

Conflict resolution: Be prepared to address frustrations constructively, focusing on maintaining the relationship and finding common ground.

Build trust-based relationships:

Deliver on promises: Consistently follow through on commitments to establish reliability and credibility.

Show empathy: Understand others' expectations and needs by placing yourself in their position.

Celebrate achievements: Acknowledge and celebrate shared successes, reinforcing collaboration and mutual trust.

Step-by-Step Guide to Applying the "Manage Expectations" Principle:

Define clear, realistic expectations: Use measurable criteria and set defined deadlines.

Communicate assertively: Be clear, concise, and respectful when discussing expectations.

Address unrealistic expectations: Negotiate, remain flexible, and communicate reasons assertively.

Build trust: Fulfill commitments, demonstrate empathy, and celebrate achievements.

Adjustments if Desired Results Are Not Achieved:

If conflicts or misunderstandings arise: Revisit the expectations set, clarify points of disagreement, and improve communication among all parties.

If expectations are unmet: Analyze the reasons for failure, adjust expectations if needed, and seek constructive solutions to resolve the issue.

If trust is broken: Take responsibility for mistakes, offer sincere apologies, and take concrete steps to rebuild trust.

Examples:

A manager defining team goals: Sets clear objectives and responsibilities for team members and provides regular performance feedback.

A couple discussing relationship expectations: Talks openly about household responsibilities, quality time together, and future plans.

A freelancer setting client expectations: Establishes clear timelines and budgets and maintains transparent communication about project progress.

Managing expectations is a practice that extends beyond communication; it reflects a commitment to clarity, empathy, and accountability. By setting realistic goals, communicating assertively, and fulfilling promises, you build strong relationships and promote a culture of collaboration and trust.

Remember, expectations are not static. As circumstances change, flexibility in renegotiating and adjusting goals is essential for maintaining alignment. The ability to navigate challenges, offer solutions, and celebrate shared achievements strengthens the dynamics of any interaction, whether personal or professional.

Practicing expectation management reduces conflicts, enhances productivity, and fosters deeper connections. Embracing this approach establishes a foundation of trust that drives positive, lasting results. Be clear, consistent, and empathetic, and witness how managing expectations transforms your relationships and achievements.

Law 32
Build Consensus

Building consensus is an indispensable skill for resolving conflicts, making effective decisions, and fostering collaboration in any setting. Whether in a workplace, community, or among nations, consensus forms the foundation for sustainable solutions that address the needs and interests of all involved. It is more than simple agreement; it is a process that strengthens relationships, sparks creativity, and nurtures trust and mutual respect.

Consensus-building begins with constructive dialogue. Creating a safe space where everyone feels comfortable sharing their ideas is essential for a productive process. Active listening and focusing on mutually beneficial solutions demonstrate respect and engagement, laying the groundwork for shared understanding.

Identifying common interests is key to consensus. By exploring diverse perspectives and finding points of agreement, you can develop options that benefit all parties, fostering a sense of collaboration and belonging. Constructively managing conflicts and facilitating communication further help overcome barriers and ensure discussions remain productive.

Building consensus isn't merely a technique; it is a commitment to cooperation and harmony. Embracing this approach allows you not only to solve problems but also to create an environment where trust, creativity, and motivation thrive.

Personal Benefits:

Conflict resolution: Consensus enables peaceful and constructive conflict resolution by finding solutions that satisfy everyone involved, avoiding disputes and disruptions.

Strengthened relationships: The process fosters trust, mutual respect, and collaboration, building stronger interpersonal connections.

Improved communication: Seeking consensus encourages open and honest dialogue, creating a space where people feel comfortable expressing their ideas and opinions.

More effective decision-making: Decisions made through consensus are more sustainable and effective, as they consider the needs and perspectives of all stakeholders.

Increased motivation and engagement: When people feel included in decision-making, their motivation and commitment rise, leading to greater productivity and success.

Creative and innovative solutions: Diverse opinions and perspectives in the consensus-building process stimulate creativity and lead to innovative solutions.

Application Methods:

Foster constructive dialogue:

Create a safe and respectful environment: Ensure everyone feels comfortable sharing ideas without fear of judgment or criticism.

Practice active listening: Pay genuine attention to others' perspectives and needs, demonstrating empathy and understanding.

Ask clarifying questions: Encourage deeper discussion by asking thoughtful questions that clarify points and encourage participation.

Stay solution-focused: Focus on finding solutions that address shared interests rather than defending individual positions.

Identify common interests:

Explore diverse viewpoints: Understand the unique needs and interests of each person or group involved.

Find areas of agreement: Identify points of convergence to use as a foundation for building consensus.

Create mutually beneficial options: Develop win-win solutions that address the concerns and objectives of all parties.

Manage conflicts constructively:

Acknowledge and validate emotions: Show empathy by recognizing and validating the feelings of those involved.

Facilitate communication: Act as a mediator, fostering respectful and productive dialogue between parties.

Seek creative solutions: Explore alternative approaches to address everyone's needs, even if they differ from initial proposals.

Cultivate a collaborative environment:

Promote trust and mutual respect: Foster a space where people feel valued and respected for their contributions.

Encourage participation: Ensure everyone has the opportunity to share their input, leveraging diverse perspectives and experiences.

Celebrate agreements and results: Recognize and honor the collective achievements, reinforcing the value of teamwork.

Step-by-Step Guide to Applying the "Build Consensus" Principle:

Foster constructive dialogue: Create a safe, respectful space, listen actively, ask clarifying questions, and focus on solutions.

Identify common interests: Explore perspectives, pinpoint areas of agreement, and develop mutually beneficial options.

Manage conflicts constructively: Validate emotions, facilitate communication, and seek creative solutions.

Cultivate collaboration: Promote trust, encourage participation, and celebrate shared successes.

Adjustments if Desired Results Are Not Achieved:

If consensus isn't reached: Review the process, identify points of disagreement, and explore new negotiation and mediation strategies.

If resistance arises: Understand the reasons behind it, engage in individual dialogue, and incorporate these perspectives into the process.

If agreements aren't honored: Reinforce the importance of accountability, and implement monitoring mechanisms to ensure commitments are upheld.

Examples:

A workplace team: Collaborates to set project goals and deadlines, building consensus on priorities and task allocation.

A community group: Discusses and decides on neighborhood improvements, reaching a consensus on shared needs and solutions.

International negotiations: Nations work together to develop environmental agreements, aligning on emission reduction goals and climate action strategies.

Building consensus is more than achieving agreement; it's about fostering connection, understanding, and collaboration. By promoting respectful dialogue, identifying common interests, and seeking creative solutions, you create an environment where people feel valued and motivated to contribute.

While achieving consensus can be challenging, the effort yields valuable rewards—stronger relationships, more effective decisions, and greater engagement. The key lies in empathy, clear communication, and openness to diverse perspectives.

By celebrating shared successes, you reinforce the importance of cooperation and inspire trust for future collaborations. Practicing consensus-building transforms challenges into opportunities and relationships into lasting partnerships, creating a positive and enduring impact.

Law 33
Lead Teams

Leading teams is one of the most challenging yet rewarding responsibilities in any professional or personal journey. An effective leader not only guides their team toward ambitious goals but also inspires, supports, and fosters an environment where every member feels valued and motivated to perform at their best.

The essence of team leadership lies in building relationships founded on trust and mutual respect. Open communication, recognizing contributions, and demonstrating empathy are key to creating genuine connections with team members. Additionally, effective leadership requires a clear vision that inspires and mobilizes people, transforming goals into a shared purpose.

Strategic delegation and empowerment are equally critical. Allowing the team autonomy to make decisions and actively contribute builds trust and promotes collaboration. Simultaneously, clear and consistent communication ensures alignment, while proactive conflict resolution maintains harmony and productivity.

Successfully leading a team demands dedication, interpersonal skills, and strategic thinking. When done well, this practice drives results and fosters personal and collective growth, leaving a lasting impact on both the leader and the team.

Personal Benefits:

Achievement of ambitious goals: Leading effective teams enables you to achieve complex objectives that are unattainable alone.

Development of leadership skills: Leadership hones essential abilities such as communication, negotiation, decision-making, conflict resolution, and motivation.

Professional growth: Successfully leading teams opens doors to career advancement, recognition, and higher-level leadership opportunities.

Increased influence: Effective leaders inspire confidence, respect, and admiration, amplifying their impact on others.

Stronger relationships: Leadership fosters strong, lasting relationships built on trust, mutual respect, and collaboration.

Personal fulfillment: Leading a successful team brings a profound sense of accomplishment and purpose.

Application Methods:

Build trust-based relationships:

Foster open communication: Engage with your team clearly, transparently, and respectfully, creating an environment where everyone feels comfortable expressing their ideas and opinions.

Demonstrate trust in your team: Delegate responsibilities and trust in each member's abilities and potential to perform their tasks effectively.

Be present and available: Take time to know each team member individually, listen to their concerns, and provide support when needed.

Recognize and value contributions: Acknowledge and celebrate individual and collective achievements, showing appreciation for the team's work.

Define a clear vision and inspire your team:

Share your vision: Clearly articulate the team's objectives and how each member's efforts contribute to the overall success.

Motivate and inspire: Use your passion and enthusiasm to ignite a sense of purpose and belonging among team members.

Lead by example: Demonstrate commitment, dedication, and ethical behavior through your actions and decisions.

Delegate responsibilities and empower the team:

Delegate effectively: Assign tasks aligned with each team member's skills and experiences, providing growth and development opportunities.

Encourage autonomy and support: Grant team members the freedom to make decisions and execute tasks independently while remaining available to offer guidance.

Promote collaboration: Foster teamwork, idea-sharing, and mutual support within the team.

Communicate clearly and effectively:

Maintain transparency: Share relevant information, feedback, and expectations in a clear and concise manner.

Practice active listening: Pay attention to the team's needs, ideas, and concerns, demonstrating empathy and understanding.

Use multiple communication channels: Ensure effective information flow through meetings, emails, instant messaging, or online platforms.

Manage conflicts and promote harmony:

Identify and resolve conflicts: Be attentive to potential conflicts and address them proactively and constructively.

Encourage collaboration and respect: Create a positive and respectful work environment where differences are embraced and valued.

Support peaceful conflict resolution: Guide the team toward resolving disagreements autonomously and constructively, offering mediation when necessary.

Step-by-Step Guide to Applying the "Lead Teams" Principle:

Build trust: Communicate openly, demonstrate confidence in your team, and recognize contributions.

Define a vision and inspire: Share a clear vision, motivate your team, and lead by example.

Delegate and empower: Assign tasks strategically, encourage autonomy, and foster collaboration.

Communicate effectively: Be transparent, listen actively, and use appropriate communication channels.

Manage conflicts: Address issues proactively, promote collaboration, and encourage constructive resolution.

Adjustments if Desired Results Are Not Achieved:

If the team lacks engagement: Reassess your leadership approach, seek feedback, and implement strategies to enhance motivation and commitment.

If conflicts persist: Identify underlying causes, implement conflict resolution strategies, and cultivate a more positive and collaborative environment.

If results fall short: Reevaluate team goals, provide training or development opportunities, and optimize workflows.

Examples:

A project leader: Inspires the team with a clear project vision, delegates responsibilities effectively, and celebrates collective successes.

A sports coach: Motivates athletes, fosters team spirit, and guides them to victory through strategic leadership.

An orchestra conductor: Leads with precision and passion, inspiring each musician to contribute their best for a harmonious and impactful performance.

Team leadership is a journey that blends strategy, empathy, and inspiration. By fostering trust, communicating a clear vision, and promoting collaboration, you create an environment where every team member thrives and contributes to collective success.

An effective leader listens, supports, and values individuals. Managing conflicts constructively and celebrating shared achievements strengthens team cohesion and inspires lasting commitment.

Leading with integrity and passion not only achieves goals but transforms a team into a motivated, cohesive force. Continue refining your leadership skills to empower your team and reach new heights. Leadership is about more than guiding—it's about building a legacy of trust, collaboration, and excellence.

Law 34
Manage Conflicts

Managing conflicts is a critical skill for building healthy relationships, fostering harmony, and achieving effective resolutions in situations of disagreement. Conflicts are inevitable wherever differing perspectives, needs, and interests coexist. However, when handled constructively, they can become opportunities for learning, innovation, and strengthening interpersonal bonds.

Effective conflict management begins with identifying its root causes. Understanding the interests and motivations behind disagreements enables all parties to find common ground and work collaboratively toward solutions. Assertive communication plays a central role, allowing needs and emotions to be expressed clearly and respectfully, while active listening fosters understanding and empathy.

Negotiating solutions that benefit all parties is key to resolving conflicts productively. This approach minimizes tension and builds an environment of collaboration and trust. Additionally, tools such as mediation and nonviolent communication can facilitate dialogue in complex situations, ensuring a respectful and balanced process.

Managing conflicts is not just a functional practice—it is a demonstration of emotional maturity and leadership. When cultivated and applied, this skill contributes to creating more peaceful, productive, and rewarding environments.

Personal Benefits

Improved relationships: Constructive conflict management strengthens relationships, building trust, mutual respect, and intimacy.

Personal and professional growth: Learning to handle conflicts healthily enhances communication, negotiation, and problem-solving skills.

Stress reduction: Effectively managing conflicts reduces the stress and anxiety associated with tense and discordant situations.

Increased productivity: Resolving conflicts constructively boosts workplace productivity by preventing wasted time and energy on unproductive disputes.

Innovative solutions: Well-managed conflicts can lead to creative and innovative solutions, as they encourage exploring new perspectives and alternatives.

Fostering peace: Conflict management contributes to creating more peaceful and harmonious environments at home, work, and in society.

Methods of Application

Identify the causes of conflict:

Analyze the situation: Delve into the root causes of the conflict by understanding the interests, needs, and perspectives of all parties involved.

Communicate openly: Engage in dialogue with the people involved, asking clarifying questions to better grasp their viewpoints.

Pinpoint disagreements: Clarify areas of contention and identify the conflicting goals causing the dispute.

Communicate assertively:

Express needs and feelings: Clearly and respectfully convey your needs, emotions, and opinions without blaming or attacking others.

Listen actively: Pay close attention to what others say, showing empathy and striving to understand their perspectives.

Maintain emotional control: Stay calm, take deep breaths, and avoid impulsive reactions during tense moments.

Negotiate mutually acceptable solutions:

Aim for win-win outcomes: Look for solutions that address the interests of all parties, ensuring everyone feels like a winner.

Be flexible and open to concessions: Be willing to compromise on certain points and consider alternative options to reach a satisfactory agreement.

Find common ground: Focus on areas of agreement and use them as a foundation to build a joint resolution.

Create an environment of respect and understanding:

Promote empathy: Encourage participants to see the situation from each other's perspectives to better understand their motivations.

Value diversity: Acknowledge and appreciate diverse opinions and viewpoints, recognizing conflict as a potential source of growth and learning.

Build communication bridges: Facilitate dialogue between parties, fostering an atmosphere where everyone feels comfortable expressing their ideas and emotions.

Use conflict resolution tools:

Mediation: In intense conflicts or when communication is strained, involve a neutral mediator to facilitate constructive dialogue and negotiation.

Negotiation: Apply negotiation techniques to reach an agreement that satisfies everyone involved.

Nonviolent communication (NVC): Practice NVC, emphasizing empathy, authentic expression of feelings, and clear, specific requests.

Step-by-Step Guide to Apply "Manage Conflicts":

Identify causes: Analyze the situation, engage in open communication, and identify key disagreements.

Communicate assertively: Express your needs, listen actively, and maintain emotional control.

Negotiate solutions: Seek win-win outcomes, remain flexible, and find common ground.

Foster respect: Promote empathy, value diversity, and build bridges for dialogue.

Utilize tools: Leverage mediation, negotiation, and nonviolent communication techniques.

Adjustments if Desired Results Are Not Achieved:

If conflicts persist: Explore alternative approaches, try different resolution techniques, or step away temporarily to reassess the situation.

If you feel intimidated or threatened: Prioritize your safety and seek support from trusted individuals or authorities.

If the conflict escalates to violence: Withdraw from the situation immediately and seek professional help to address trauma and prevent recurrence.

Examples:

Workplace disagreement: Two colleagues disagree on how to execute a project. They hold a meeting to openly share their ideas, listen to each other's arguments, and develop a solution that incorporates both perspectives.

Relationship conflict: A couple facing a relationship crisis seeks help from a therapist to improve communication, resolve conflicts constructively, and strengthen their bond.

International dispute: Two nations in conflict over territorial issues begin negotiations mediated by an international organization, aiming for a peaceful and lasting resolution.

Managing conflicts is an art requiring empathy, communication, and a willingness to find solutions that address everyone's needs. By identifying root causes, communicating assertively, and striving for win-win resolutions, you can turn tension into growth and understanding.

Conflicts handled well not only resolve immediate issues but also strengthen relationships and encourage respect and collaboration. Embrace diversity of thought as a source of learning and innovation, approaching disagreements with openness and dialogue.

Practicing conflict management fosters harmony and builds deeper connections in all areas of life. By adopting this practice, you demonstrate leadership and emotional maturity, creating positive impacts in both personal and professional interactions. Turn conflict into an opportunity for unity rather than division.

Law 35
Promote Collaboration

Promoting collaboration is fundamental to creating productive, innovative, and harmonious environments. Collaboration goes beyond simple teamwork; it involves integrating diverse perspectives, skills, and ideas into a collective effort to achieve shared goals. When people collaborate effectively, they not only overcome challenges more easily but also generate creative and impactful results.

A culture of collaboration begins with building trust and fostering transparent communication. Creating an environment where people feel respected, valued, and encouraged to share their ideas is key to collaborative success. Additionally, embracing diversity in experiences and skills enriches discussions and leads to innovative solutions.

Modern tools and technologies further enhance collaboration, enabling teams to work together seamlessly, regardless of physical location. Brainstorming sessions, communication platforms, and project management tools make collaborative efforts more dynamic and efficient.

Promoting collaboration is not just a strategy to boost productivity but also a way to strengthen interpersonal bonds and foster a culture of continuous learning. When individuals feel part of a collective effort, they become more engaged, motivated, and committed to the group's success.

Personal Benefits

Increased productivity and efficiency: Collaboration enables tasks to be shared, skills to be utilized optimally, and duplication of efforts to be avoided.

More creative and innovative solutions: Diverse perspectives and experiences stimulate creativity and lead to more effective and original solutions.

Improved communication and relationships: Collaboration encourages open communication and constructive dialogue, strengthening interpersonal relationships and creating a positive work environment.

Development of interpersonal skills: Working collaboratively enhances essential interpersonal skills such as communication, negotiation, empathy, and leadership.

Higher motivation and engagement: Collaboration fosters a sense of belonging and purpose, increasing individual motivation and engagement.

Building a culture of sharing and learning: Collaboration promotes the sharing of knowledge and continuous learning, benefiting all involved.

Methods of Application

Build a culture of collaboration:

Transparent communication: Create an environment of open, honest, and transparent communication to encourage dialogue and information exchange.

Trust and mutual respect: Foster trust and respect among team members, ensuring everyone feels comfortable expressing their ideas and opinions.

Value diversity: Recognize and appreciate diverse skills, experiences, and perspectives, leveraging them to enrich collaborative processes and solutions.

Celebrate collective successes: Recognize and celebrate team accomplishments, reinforcing the importance of working together.

Encourage communication and idea-sharing:

Brainstorming and creative sessions: Facilitate brainstorming sessions and activities that encourage group creativity and idea generation.

Effective communication platforms: Use tools like instant messaging, video conferencing, and project management platforms to facilitate idea exchange and communication.

Knowledge and experience sharing: Encourage team members to share their expertise and best practices through workshops, presentations, or mentoring.

Leverage tools and technologies for collaboration:

Project management tools: Utilize tools that allow teams to plan, organize, track, and execute tasks collaboratively and transparently.

Online collaboration platforms: Explore platforms that enable real-time document sharing, simultaneous editing, and seamless communication.

Corporate social networks: Use internal social networks to facilitate communication, share information, and build a collaborative community.

Step-by-Step Guide to Apply "Promote Collaboration":

Build a culture of collaboration: Communicate transparently, foster trust, value diversity, and celebrate successes.

Encourage communication and sharing: Promote brainstorming, use effective communication platforms, and encourage knowledge sharing.

Use tools and technologies: Employ project management tools, online collaboration platforms, and corporate social networks to streamline teamwork.

Adjustments if Desired Results Are Not Achieved:

If collaboration is low: Identify barriers such as lack of trust, ineffective communication, or unclear objectives. Take steps to address these issues and foster a more collaborative environment.

If conflicts arise within the team: Act as a mediator to facilitate communication and find solutions that meet everyone's needs.

If tools are not used effectively: Provide training and support to ensure team members understand and utilize collaboration tools fully.

Examples:

Development team: A software development team collaborates using an online platform to share code, test functionalities, and communicate in real-time.

Marketing team: A marketing group conducts a brainstorming session for a new campaign, using a virtual whiteboard to record and organize ideas.

Community project: A neighborhood community organizes through an online group to plan and implement local improvement projects, like building a park or hosting a cultural event.

Promoting collaboration is a powerful force that transforms individuals into cohesive and effective teams. By fostering trust, valuing diversity, and leveraging tools that facilitate teamwork, you create the ideal conditions for people to achieve more together than they ever could alone.

The key to successful collaboration lies in open communication, idea-sharing, and celebrating team achievements. Every collective victory strengthens the spirit of unity and motivates members to contribute with enthusiasm.

Embracing collaboration is not just about meeting goals; it's about building lasting connections, creating a culture of mutual growth, and turning individual efforts into extraordinary accomplishments. Incorporate collaboration as a principle in your personal and professional life, and watch it transform challenges into opportunities and efforts into remarkable successes.

Law 36
Celebrate Achievements

Celebrating achievements is a vital practice for maintaining motivation, boosting self-esteem, and fostering a culture of positivity and recognition. In a world often focused on the next challenge, taking time to acknowledge efforts and celebrate milestones is essential. This simple act can transform how we view progress and deepen our connections with others.

Acknowledging accomplishments—whether personal or collective—has profound effects. For individuals, it reinforces confidence and belief in their abilities. For teams, it strengthens bonds, promotes collaboration, and cultivates a sense of value and belonging. Celebrating also nurtures gratitude—for opportunities, the people who support us, and the journey itself.

Celebrations don't need to be grand to be meaningful. Small gestures, such as sincere compliments, simple rewards, or shared moments of reflection, can have a significant impact. The key is to make recognition a regular habit, incorporating it into daily routines and using every victory as a stepping stone to new goals.

Celebrating achievements is more than a festive moment; it's a way to consolidate lessons, renew motivation, and inspire future actions. By embracing this habit, you strengthen your personal and collective journey, turning each victory into a bridge to greater accomplishments.

Personal Benefits

Increased motivation: Celebrating achievements keeps motivation high, reinforcing a sense of progress and encouraging pursuit of new challenges.

Boosted self-esteem: Recognizing your own successes and receiving acknowledgment from others builds confidence and belief in your capabilities.

Enhanced relationships: Celebrating others' accomplishments strengthens bonds, fostering an environment of support, recognition, and positivity.

Cultivation of gratitude: Celebrating victories promotes gratitude for opportunities, support systems, and accomplishments.

Fostering a positive culture: Recognizing successes contributes to a motivating and uplifting atmosphere in both personal and professional settings.

Improved happiness and well-being: Taking time to honor successes enhances feelings of happiness, fulfillment, and life satisfaction.

Methods of Application

Recognize your own successes:

Keep a journal of achievements: Record your accomplishments, big or small, to reflect on your progress.

Reward yourself: Treat yourself to something enjoyable, such as a gift, a trip, or a relaxing activity when you achieve a goal.

Share your accomplishments: Celebrate by sharing your successes with friends, family, or colleagues for additional recognition and encouragement.

Value others' achievements:

Offer sincere compliments: Acknowledge others' efforts and accomplishments with genuine praise.

Celebrate together: Organize small celebrations for team achievements, like a special lunch or a casual gathering.

Create a recognition environment: Implement workplace recognition programs, such as employee of the month or achievement walls.

Build a culture of celebration:

Incorporate celebrations into routines: Regularly celebrate both major milestones and smaller progress points.

Host events and activities: Organize occasions to honor special dates, milestones, and significant accomplishments.

Use symbols and rituals: Incorporate tokens like trophies, certificates, and thank-you notes to mark achievements meaningfully.

Transform victories into momentum for the future:

Reflect and learn: After celebrating, consider the journey, lessons learned, and factors contributing to success.

Renew motivation: Use the energy from the celebration to tackle new challenges with enthusiasm.

Share experiences: Inspire and motivate others by sharing your stories of success.

Step-by-Step Guide to Applying "Celebrate Achievements":

Recognize your own successes: Keep a journal, reward yourself, and share your accomplishments.

Value others' achievements: Offer compliments, celebrate together, and create recognition opportunities.

Build a celebration culture: Make celebrations routine, organize events, and use meaningful symbols.

Transform victories into momentum: Reflect on successes, reignite motivation, and inspire others with your story.

Adjustments if Desired Results Are Not Achieved:

If you struggle to recognize your achievements: Practice self-compassion, identify your strengths, and celebrate even small victories.

If motivation doesn't follow celebrations: Reassess your goals, set inspiring challenges, and create an actionable plan to pursue them.

If a culture of celebration doesn't develop: Emphasize the importance of recognition, introduce new celebration methods, and lead by example in honoring successes.

Examples:

Sales team: A sales team that meets its monthly target celebrates with a special dinner.

Athlete: An athlete commemorates a competition win with family and friends.

Company: A business organizes an event to celebrate its anniversary and recognizes employees' contributions.

Celebrating achievements offers an opportunity to acknowledge effort, appreciate progress, and strengthen connections. Whether in personal or professional settings, this act creates a positive cycle of motivation and fulfillment, demonstrating that every step forward deserves recognition.

By acknowledging your own victories, you build confidence and prepare for new challenges. By celebrating others' successes, you strengthen relationships and encourage collaboration. Incorporating celebrations into your routine fosters a culture of positivity and growth, making the journey toward your goals more rewarding.

Remember that every achievement, no matter how small, is a significant milestone in your journey. Celebrate, reflect on your accomplishments, and use that energy to aim for new horizons. Recognizing what has been achieved is as important as planning for what's ahead. Make celebration a constant practice and turn your victories into fuel for a richer, more meaningful life.

Law 37
Provide Feedback

Providing feedback is a powerful tool for fostering personal and professional growth, enhancing relationships, and cultivating a continuous learning environment. When delivered clearly, respectfully, and constructively, feedback inspires positive change, acknowledges efforts, and corrects deviations, benefiting both the giver and the receiver.

Effective feedback goes beyond pointing out mistakes or offering praise. It should be objective, focused on specific behaviors, and grounded in clear observations. Striking a balance between positive reinforcement and improvement suggestions is essential to ensure the message is well-received and impactful.

Creating an open and safe dialogue strengthens trust, fosters collaboration, and develops interpersonal skills like communication, empathy, and active listening. These skills are indispensable for leaders, educators, and professionals across various fields.

When paired with ongoing support and progress monitoring, feedback evolves from an information exchange to a practice of mentorship and development. This approach ensures suggestions are implemented and advancements recognized, creating a positive cycle of growth and learning.

Personal Benefits

Performance improvement: Constructive feedback helps identify strengths and areas for improvement, enabling skill development and enhanced performance.

Increased motivation: Recognizing good work and encouraging improvement inspires greater dedication and excellence.

Strengthened relationships: Offering sincere and respectful feedback builds trust and collaboration in interpersonal relationships.

Leadership development: The ability to give effective feedback is a key trait of leaders who inspire and guide team growth.

Enhanced communication: The process of giving and receiving feedback sharpens communication skills and promotes open dialogue.

Continuous learning culture: Regular feedback fosters an environment of ongoing improvement and mutual growth.

Methods of Application

Prepare to Provide Feedback:

Define the purpose: Clarify the goal of your feedback—whether to recognize achievements, address errors, suggest improvements, or guide development.

Gather specific information: Base your feedback on concrete facts and observations, avoiding generalizations and personal judgments.

Choose the right time and place: Deliver feedback at an appropriate time when the person is receptive, in a private and comfortable setting.

Communicate Clearly and Objectively:

Focus on observable behaviors: Describe specific behaviors and their impact rather than making subjective judgments.

Use clear and direct language: Avoid jargon or vague expressions; be concise and straightforward.

Address behaviors, not the person: Keep feedback targeted at actions or behaviors without personal criticism or labels.

Offer Constructive Feedback:

Balance positives and negatives: Start by acknowledging strengths before addressing areas needing improvement.

Focus on development: Provide actionable, specific suggestions for improvement and skill growth.

Show empathy and support: Demonstrate care for the person's progress and offer your assistance in achieving their goals.

Encourage Dialogue and Active Listening:

Ask open-ended questions: Invite the individual to share their thoughts, concerns, and perspectives on the feedback.

Listen attentively: Pay close attention to their responses, showing respect and empathy.

Be open to discussion: Be willing to adjust your approach based on their feedback and engage in constructive dialogue.

Monitor Progress and Offer Continued Support:

Set clear next steps: Collaboratively outline actionable steps for implementing feedback.

Provide ongoing support and mentorship: Be available to guide and support their development journey.

Recognize progress: Acknowledge improvements and provide further feedback as needed.

Step-by-Step Guide to Applying "Provide Feedback":

Prepare: Define your objective, gather information, and choose the right time and place.

Communicate clearly: Be specific, objective, and focus on behaviors.

Offer constructive feedback: Balance positives and negatives, emphasize development, and show empathy.

Encourage dialogue: Ask open questions, listen actively, and foster discussion.

Monitor progress: Set actionable steps, offer support, and recognize improvements.

Adjustments if Desired Results Are Not Achieved:

If the person reacts defensively: Stay calm, reaffirm your positive intent, and focus on collaborative problem-solving.

If they show disinterest in change: Emphasize the feedback's importance for growth and provide resources to facilitate improvement.

If offering negative feedback feels uncomfortable: Practice communication skills, rely on facts, and remember that constructive feedback drives growth.

Examples:

A manager praises an employee for excellent project execution while suggesting ways to enhance presentation skills.

A teacher provides written feedback on a student's essay, highlighting strengths and suggesting improvements in structure and argumentation.

A friend offers honest feedback about another's behavior to help improve their relationships.

Providing feedback is an art that requires clarity, empathy, and a genuine desire to foster growth. Balancing recognition of strengths with actionable suggestions for improvement creates opportunities for individuals to reach their full potential.

Feedback is more than criticism or praise—it's a conversation that builds trust and strengthens connections. Open dialogue and consistent follow-ups ensure feedback is effectively implemented and progress acknowledged.

By practicing the art of feedback, you refine your communication and leadership skills while contributing to a culture of respect, learning, and collaboration. Offer feedback with sincerity and intention, and watch it transform both performance and relationships for the better.

Law 38
Inspire Action

Inspiring action is the ability to turn ideas into reality and dreams into achievements. Whether in a personal, professional, or social context, mobilizing others to take meaningful steps is a hallmark of effective leaders and visionaries. By inspiring action, you motivate people to pursue ambitious goals and create a lasting positive impact on their lives and communities.

A purposeful communication strategy is the foundation for inspiring action. By articulating a clear and passionate vision, telling compelling stories, and using persuasive language, you ignite enthusiasm and commitment. However, inspiration transcends words; leading by example is critical. Demonstrating dedication, acting consistently, and sharing your journey establishes trust and admiration, providing a model for others to emulate.

Building genuine connections is another key element. Showing empathy, valuing individual talents, and offering support strengthen interpersonal bonds and create an environment where people feel motivated and appreciated. Empowering others with autonomy and responsibility unlocks their potential, transforming a group into a collective force aligned with a greater purpose.

Inspiring action is not just about achieving goals; it's about awakening in people the desire and courage to make a difference. This skill turns challenges into opportunities and teams into engaged communities, creating an impact that resonates far beyond the present.

Personal Benefits

Achievement of objectives: Inspiring action enhances the likelihood of turning ideas into reality and reaching ambitious goals, whether personal, professional, or social.

High-performing teams: Leaders who inspire create motivated, engaged, and productive teams, driving collective success.

Enhanced influence and leadership: The ability to inspire strengthens your leadership and influence, making you a reference for those around you.

Stronger relationships: Inspiring action fosters trust, mutual respect, and purpose-driven relationships.

Personal growth and skill development: Inspiring others sharpens communication, leadership, persuasion, and emotional intelligence.

Positive impact: Motivating action creates meaningful contributions to causes and builds a better future.

Methods of Application

Communicate with Purpose:

Define a clear and inspiring vision: Share a concise vision that sparks passion and demonstrates how collective actions contribute to a larger goal.

Use persuasive language: Employ powerful, emotive, and relatable language that resonates with the audience's values and aspirations.

Tell impactful stories: Share real-life, inspiring stories that illustrate the power of action and its positive outcomes.

Communicate authentically: Convey your passion and commitment genuinely, creating a connection through authenticity.

Lead by Example:

Demonstrate commitment: Take the first step and show unwavering dedication to the cause, inspiring others through your actions.

Be a role model: Embody the values and behaviors you wish to see in others, earning their trust and admiration.

Share your journey: Speak openly about your successes and setbacks, emphasizing that action and perseverance lead to results.

Create Genuine Connections:

Show empathy and genuine interest: Connect with people personally by showing empathy and understanding their stories and perspectives.

Build trust-based relationships: Foster trust, respect, and collaboration, creating a safe space for people to act and contribute.

Offer support and recognition: Acknowledge and celebrate contributions, ensuring individuals feel valued and motivated.

Unlock Potential:

Identify and value individual talents: Recognize the unique skills of each person, offering opportunities to channel their strengths toward collective goals.

Delegate and empower: Grant autonomy and responsibility, encouraging individuals to take initiative and lead change.

Foster growth and learning: Create an environment where challenges encourage growth, learning, and maximizing potential.

Step-by-Step Guide to Apply "Inspire Action":

Communicate with Purpose: Define a compelling vision, use persuasive language, share stories, and maintain authenticity.

Lead by Example: Act first, model desired behaviors, and share personal experiences.

Build Genuine Connections: Show empathy, establish trust, and provide recognition.

Unlock Potential: Identify talents, delegate responsibilities, and encourage growth.

Adjustments if Desired Results Are Not Achieved:

If people are not motivated to act: Review your communication strategy, seek feedback, and adjust your message to better connect with their needs and aspirations.

If resistance or disengagement arises: Identify the root causes, open a dialogue, and co-create solutions that address concerns.

If you feel demotivated or doubted: Revisit your purpose, reconnect with your passion, and draw inspiration from role models and success stories.

Examples:

A community leader mobilizing neighbors to revitalize their neighborhood by sharing a vision of a brighter future and leading by example.

A teacher igniting a love for learning in students by creating an engaging and challenging classroom environment.

An entrepreneur inspiring a team to innovate by sharing their vision for groundbreaking products and motivating them to exceed their limits.

Inspiring action is a journey requiring purpose, authenticity, and dedication. By articulating an inspiring vision, leading by example, and fostering genuine connections, you lay the groundwork to transform motivation into movement and potential into achievement.

Remember, inspiration is contagious. Each action rooted in a clear purpose has the power to influence and engage others, creating a ripple effect of positive change. Celebrate individual contributions, honor collective achievements, and cultivate an environment where growth and collaboration thrive.

When you inspire action, you not only drive results but also leave a legacy of leadership, empathy, and transformation. Be the force that moves people and ideas toward a brighter future, and witness the profound impact of your actions on the world around you.

Law 39
Build a Legacy

Building a legacy means living in a way that your impact continues to influence lives, even after you're gone. Beyond personal achievements, creating a legacy entails leaving a lasting positive mark on society, inspiring values, actions, and changes that transcend time.

This journey begins by defining your core values and purpose. Self-awareness is essential to identify what truly matters and how your actions can contribute to a greater cause. Living according to these principles creates consistency and meaning, guiding your path toward significant impact.

Your legacy is deeply connected to your passions and talents. By investing in what you love and honing your skills, you can make unique contributions to the world. Engaging in causes aligned with your values and genuinely connecting with your community allows you to transform lives and inspire others to follow suit.

Creating something that endures—whether it's a piece of art, an idea, or a life example—is one of the most powerful ways to establish a legacy. Sharing knowledge, building lasting relationships, and leaving tangible marks ensure that your influence continues into the future.

Building a legacy is not only an act of generosity but also a journey of purpose and personal fulfillment. It reflects not just what you achieved but also the impact you had on people and the world around you.

Personal Benefits

Purpose and Meaning: Striving to build a legacy gives your life direction and significance, shaping your decisions toward a greater goal.

Positive Impact: Creating a legacy allows you to make a difference, leaving the world better than you found it.

Transcendence: Your legacy extends beyond your lifetime, influencing lives and inspiring others for generations.

Recognition and Admiration: A lasting legacy earns respect and appreciation, both during your life and after.

Inspiration to Others: Your legacy motivates others to live purposefully and pursue their own dreams and goals.

Connection to Humanity: Building a legacy ties you to the broader human story and the future of society, fostering a sense of belonging to something greater than yourself.

Methods of Application

Define Your Values and Purpose:

Self-awareness: Reflect on your values, beliefs, and principles, identifying what truly drives your actions.

Life Purpose: Articulate your mission in life and the impact you want to create in the world.

Values in Action: Align your daily actions with your principles to ensure consistency and integrity.

Identify Your Passions and Talents:

Explore Interests: Dedicate time to discovering hobbies and activities that ignite your passion.

Develop Skills: Recognize your natural talents and invest in mastering them to create meaningful contributions.

Trust Your Intuition: Follow your instincts to choose paths and projects that resonate with your values.

Contribute to a Cause Greater Than Yourself:

Find Your Cause: Identify a cause that inspires you to act and make a difference in the world.

Engage with Your Community: Actively participate in social projects or initiatives that uplift your community.

Impact Lives Positively: Focus on inspiring, supporting, and transforming the lives of those around you.

Create Something Enduring:

Share Knowledge and Experiences: Write a book, start a blog, record videos, or give talks to disseminate your insights.

Build Something Lasting: Create a business, develop a product, or produce art that stands the test of time.

Invest in Personal Growth: Continually learn, evolve, and enrich yourself to ensure your legacy reflects wisdom and fulfillment.

Step-by-Step Guide to "Build a Legacy":

Define Your Values and Purpose: Engage in self-reflection, define your mission, and align your actions with your values.

Discover Passions and Talents: Explore your interests, develop your skills, and trust your instincts.

Contribute to a Greater Cause: Find a cause, connect with your community, and impact lives positively.

Create Something Timeless: Share your knowledge, build enduring contributions, and commit to personal growth.

Adjustments if Desired Results Are Not Achieved:

If you feel lost or directionless: Revisit your values, seek inspiration from role models, and experiment with new experiences to identify your passions.

If leaving a mark seems challenging: Focus on making a difference in small, meaningful ways that can grow over time.

If you feel unmotivated or doubtful: Reconnect with your purpose, find inspiration in stories of impactful people, and take one step at a time.

Examples:

A Teacher: Who dedicates their life to educating and inspiring students, leaving a legacy of knowledge and transformation.

An Artist: Who creates works that resonate across generations, evoking emotions and sparking thought.

An Entrepreneur: Who builds a company that generates jobs, supports the economy, and improves lives in their community.

Building a legacy is about living intentionally to leave the world better than you found it. By aligning actions with your values, nurturing your talents, and contributing to causes larger than yourself, you create an impact that transcends your lifetime.

A legacy isn't defined solely by monumental achievements; small acts of kindness, inspiration, and generosity are equally transformative. Every life you touch, idea you share, and contribution you make adds to a meaningful narrative.

As you build your legacy, you discover purpose, fulfillment, and a connection to humanity's broader story. Your influence inspires others to continue your work, creating a ripple effect of positivity. Live with intention, create with love, and leave a lasting heritage of impact and meaning.

Law 40
Take Risks

Taking risks invites you to step out of your comfort zone and explore the endless possibilities life offers. Although often feared, risk-taking is a catalyst for growth, innovation, and personal fulfillment. Embracing uncertainty and overcoming the fear of failure opens doors to opportunities that can transform your journey and take you to places you never imagined.

The process of taking risks begins with thoughtful analysis. Identifying opportunities, understanding challenges, and weighing potential rewards help you make informed, strategic decisions. While the fear of failure is a natural companion on this path, it can be reframed as a chance to learn and grow.

By consciously and progressively taking risks, you build self-confidence, resilience, and creativity. Each step into the unknown strengthens your skills and broadens your perspective. Moreover, the courage to face challenges inspires others around you, creating a ripple effect that magnifies the impact of your actions.

More than an act of bravery, taking risks is a choice of authenticity and freedom. It's saying "yes" to your dreams and working to make them a reality, despite uncertainties. This practice not only unlocks achievements but also enriches your life with valuable and meaningful experiences.

Personal Benefits

Growth and Development: Stepping out of your comfort zone and tackling new challenges fosters personal growth and the development of new skills.

Discovery of Opportunities: Taking risks opens doors to opportunities you never imagined, expanding your horizons and creating paths to success and fulfillment.

Increased Self-Confidence: Overcoming fear and successfully taking risks strengthens your belief in your ability to achieve your goals.

Innovation and Creativity: Exploring new paths and experimenting stimulate innovation and original solutions, helping you stand out in a competitive world.

Greater Resilience: Learning to manage risks and potential failures boosts your resilience and ability to overcome adversity, making you stronger and more prepared.

Authentic Living: Risk-taking aligned with your dreams allows you to live a more genuine life, reflecting your values and purpose.

Methods of Application

Identify and Evaluate Risks:

Analyze Opportunities: Carefully assess opportunities involving risks, aligning them with your goals, values, and potential outcomes.

Pinpoint Potential Risks: Realistically evaluate obstacles and losses you may encounter.

Weigh Potential Benefits: Consider the rewards, such as personal growth, new opportunities, recognition, or fulfilling dreams.

Calculate Risks and Benefits:

Assess Risk-to-Reward Ratio: Determine if the potential benefits justify the risks involved.

Prepare Contingency Plans: Plan for setbacks and challenges to minimize losses and maximize success.

Break Risks into Steps: Divide large risks into manageable stages to monitor progress and make adjustments.

Overcome Fear of Failure:

Reframe Failure: View failure as a learning opportunity and a stepping stone to growth.

Build Resilience: Cultivate the ability to recover from setbacks and move forward stronger.

Focus on Strengths: Draw confidence from your skills, talents, and positive experiences.

Take Control and Act:

Make Informed Decisions: Take responsibility for your choices and accept the consequences.

Start Small: Begin with smaller risks and gradually take on greater challenges as your confidence grows.

Don't Let Fear Hold You Back: Resist letting fear of failure keep you from pursuing dreams or exploring opportunities.

Step-by-Step Guide to "Take Risks":

Identify and Evaluate: Analyze opportunities, identify potential risks, and assess rewards.

Calculate Risks: Weigh risks against benefits, prepare contingency plans, and break risks into manageable steps.

Overcome Fear: Reframe failure, develop resilience, and focus on your strengths.

Act: Take responsibility, start small, and move forward with courage.

Adjustments if Desired Results Are Not Achieved:

In Case of Loss or Failure: Reflect on the situation, learn from your mistakes, and use the experience as a springboard for growth.

If Fear Paralyzes You: Seek support from trusted individuals, develop strategies to manage anxiety, and recall past successes.

If Opportunities Are Hard to Identify: Broaden your horizons, connect with people from diverse fields, and remain open to new experiences.

Examples:

An Entrepreneur: Invests capital in starting a new business, facing potential failure but with the chance to achieve success and fulfill a dream.

An Artist: Showcases their work to the public, risking criticism but gaining the possibility of appreciation and recognition.

A Career Changer: Leaves a stable job to pursue a passion, risking uncertainty but opening the door to a more fulfilling career.

Taking risks is a journey of self-discovery and growth. Each challenge faced and fear overcome enhances your ability to achieve what once seemed impossible. This practice doesn't eliminate fear but transforms it into a motivating force that drives your progress.

Remember, risk-taking isn't about recklessness but about seeking opportunities aligned with your values and dreams. By calculating risks, planning wisely, and acting with courage, you turn uncertainties into possibilities and setbacks into valuable lessons.

Along the way, you not only reap the rewards of your choices but also inspire others to follow their dreams. Risk-taking isn't just about achieving goals; it's a way of living authentically, embracing the new, and exploring the best that life has to offer.

Law 41
Embrace Uncertainty

Embracing uncertainty means acknowledging that life is inherently unpredictable and full of surprises. The relentless pursuit of control and predictability often prevents us from fully experiencing the richness life offers. By accepting the unknown as a constant, we make room for new opportunities, personal growth, and a more authentic, lighthearted existence.

Uncertainty, while challenging, can be a powerful ally. It invites us to leave our comfort zones, spark creativity, and explore uncharted paths. Facing the unknown requires flexibility and resilience—qualities essential for navigating life's inevitable changes. When we stop resisting uncertainty and learn to flow with it, we become more adaptable, innovative, and confident.

Accepting unpredictability helps us focus on the present moment. Instead of worrying about what we can't control, we channel our energy into what we can do now. This approach frees us from the weight of unrealistic expectations and allows us to find joy and purpose in everyday moments.

Embracing uncertainty is a practice that transforms challenges into opportunities and obstacles into lessons. It teaches us that even without guarantees, we can create, explore, and thrive.

Personal Benefits

Reduced Anxiety: Accepting uncertainty as a natural part of life reduces the stress and anxiety caused by the constant need for control.

Increased Flexibility: Embracing uncertainty develops your adaptability, helping you navigate changes with ease and resilience.

Openness to Opportunities: Uncertainty reveals possibilities and opportunities you might not notice if you stick rigidly to a plan.

Boosted Creativity: Uncertainty challenges you to think outside the box and develop innovative solutions, unlocking your creative potential.

Strengthened Intuition: Trusting your instincts becomes easier when you embrace uncertainty, guiding you through the unknown.

Lighter, More Spontaneous Living: Letting go of excessive control enables you to live with more joy, spontaneity, and authenticity.

Methods of Application

Cultivate a Flexible Mindset:

Let Go of Control: Accept that you cannot control every aspect of life and that uncertainty is a natural part of the human experience.

Adapt to Change: Be open to altering plans, adjusting strategies, and revising expectations as circumstances evolve.

See Challenges as Opportunities: Approach uncertainty as a chance to learn, grow, and discover new possibilities.

Develop Adaptability:

Practice Improvisation: Learn to respond creatively to unexpected situations without rigidly clinging to predetermined plans.

Foster Curiosity: Keep an open mind and explore the unknown with curiosity and interest.

Build Resilience: Strengthen your ability to recover from setbacks, learn from mistakes, and move forward with greater wisdom.

Embrace the Unknown:

Explore New Possibilities: Be willing to explore opportunities that differ from your initial plans or push you beyond your comfort zone.

Trust Your Intuition: Tune into your inner voice and instincts, even when there are no guarantees.

Live in the Moment: Focus on the present, appreciating each experience and allowing life to surprise you.

Turn Uncertainty into an Ally:

Find Opportunities in Chaos: Recognize that uncertainty can create space for opportunities and solutions that would not arise in a predictable environment.

Leverage Uncertainty for Innovation: Use the need to adapt as a driver for innovation and new ideas.

Build Self-Confidence: Remember past successes in uncertain situations and trust your ability to handle future challenges.

Step-by-Step Guide to "Embrace Uncertainty":

Cultivate Flexibility: Let go of control, adapt to changes, and view challenges as opportunities.

Develop Adaptability: Practice improvisation, foster curiosity, and strengthen resilience.

Embrace the Unknown: Explore possibilities, trust your intuition, and live in the moment.

Make Uncertainty Your Ally: Seek opportunities, use it to fuel innovation, and build self-confidence.

Adjustments if Desired Results Are Not Achieved:

If You Feel Anxious or Stressed About Uncertainty: Practice relaxation and mindfulness techniques to calm your mind and focus on the present.

If Adapting to Change Is Difficult: Identify the root causes of resistance to change, develop coping strategies, and seek support from trusted individuals.

If Uncertainty Paralyzes You: Recall past successes, focus on your strengths, and take small steps toward your goals without needing all the answers.

Examples:

An Entrepreneur: Adjusting their business model during an economic crisis, finding new opportunities, and turning uncertainty into a competitive advantage.

An Artist: Experimenting with new forms of creative expression, embracing the uncertainty of the creative process, and discovering fresh artistic paths.

A Traveler: Venturing to an unfamiliar country without a fixed itinerary, embracing the adventure, and enjoying the surprises of an unplanned journey.

Final Thoughts

Embrace uncertainty as an inevitable companion on your journey. Instead of resisting it, view it as an opportunity for growth, innovation, and discovery. Accepting that not everything can be controlled frees you from the burden of perfection and opens the door to richer, more meaningful experiences.

Uncertainty also provides a chance to trust in yourself and your ability to adapt and overcome challenges. Each unexpected situation can become an opportunity to learn and a springboard for new horizons.

Live lightly, exploring the unknown with curiosity and enthusiasm. By embracing uncertainty, you not only uncover new possibilities but also discover a renewed sense of freedom and authenticity, turning the unpredictable into an invitation to a more vibrant and fulfilling life.

Law 42
Cultivate Self-Awareness

Self-awareness is the foundation of an authentic and fulfilling life. It connects you to your emotions, values, and aspirations, allowing you to live more in alignment with your true self. Knowing yourself goes beyond identifying preferences—it involves understanding your reactions, behavior patterns, strengths, and areas for improvement. This journey is essential for making conscious decisions, building healthy relationships, and fostering solid self-esteem.

When you invest in self-awareness, you gain clarity about your goals and learn to manage your emotions wisely. This makes you more resilient in the face of challenges and better equipped to grow both personally and professionally. Additionally, by knowing yourself better, you enhance your ability to communicate empathetically and authentically, fostering more meaningful connections with others.

Self-awareness requires introspection, acceptance of imperfections, and openness to new perspectives. Through practices like meditation, journaling, or seeking feedback from trusted individuals, you empower yourself to live with greater freedom and purpose. By exploring your inner world, you pave the way for transformation and a more balanced and fulfilling life.

Personal Benefits

More Conscious Decision-Making: Self-awareness helps you make decisions aligned with your values, goals, and life purpose, avoiding impulsive choices or external influences.

Better Emotion Management: Understanding your emotions and triggers enables you to manage them more effectively, avoiding extreme reactions and fostering healthier relationships.

Increased Self-Esteem: Accepting your strengths and imperfections with self-compassion boosts self-esteem and promotes a positive self-image.

Improved Relationships: Self-awareness allows you to communicate more authentically and empathetically, building stronger and more meaningful relationships.

Personal and Professional Growth: Recognizing your strengths and weaknesses helps you focus on skill development and reaching your full potential.

Greater Well-Being and Happiness: Self-awareness contributes to a more authentic, balanced, and joyful life aligned with your deepest values and purposes.

Methods of Application

Connect with Yourself:

Introspection: Set aside time for self-reflection, exploring your thoughts, feelings, and experiences. Ask yourself: Who am I? What makes me happy? What are my values?

Meditation and Mindfulness: Practice meditation and mindfulness to calm your mind, connect with the present moment, and observe your thoughts and emotions without judgment.

Journaling: Keep a journal to record your thoughts, feelings, dreams, and experiences, creating a space for reflection and self-discovery.

Identify Behavior Patterns:

Observe Your Reactions: Pay attention to how you react to different situations, people, and emotions. What patterns emerge? What triggers them?

Analyze Relationships: Reflect on recurring patterns in your relationships. What types of people do you attract? How do you behave in these dynamics?

Recognize Strengths and Weaknesses: Acknowledge your skills, talents, and positive qualities, as well as your limitations and areas for improvement.

Accept Your Imperfections:

Practice Self-Compassion: Be kind and understanding with yourself, accepting your imperfections and recognizing that everyone has limitations and makes mistakes.

Let Go of Perfectionism: Free yourself from the constant pursuit of perfection, which can lead to frustration and excessive self-criticism.

Focus on Progress: Value your progress and achievements, no matter how small, and celebrate each step taken on your journey of self-awareness.

Seek Feedback and New Perspectives:

Ask Trusted People for Feedback: Talk to people who know you well and ask for honest feedback on how they see you and perceive your behavior.

Consider Different Perspectives: Be open to hearing different points of view and exploring new perspectives about yourself.

Seek Professional Help: If you face challenges in your self-awareness journey, consider seeking guidance from a therapist or counselor.

Step-by-Step Guide to "Cultivate Self-Awareness":

Connect with Yourself: Engage in introspection, meditate, and write in a journal.

Identify Patterns: Observe your reactions, analyze your relationships, and recognize your strengths and weaknesses.

Accept Imperfections: Practice self-compassion, let go of perfectionism, and focus on progress.

Seek Feedback: Ask trusted individuals for input, consider new perspectives, and seek professional help if needed.

Adjustments if Desired Results Are Not Achieved:

Difficulty Connecting with Yourself: Try different relaxation and meditation techniques, and create a calm environment for introspection.

Resistance to Accepting Imperfections: Remember that everyone has strengths and flaws, and self-acceptance is the first step toward growth.

Hesitation in Seeking Feedback: Start by asking for input from trusted individuals you feel comfortable with, and gradually expand your circle of confidants.

Examples:

Daily Meditation: A person meditates regularly to connect with their emotions and thoughts while maintaining a journal to capture insights.

Professional Feedback: An employee seeks feedback from colleagues and supervisors to identify strengths and areas for development, creating a personal growth plan.

Open Communication in Relationships: A couple shares their feelings, needs, and expectations openly, fostering a stronger and more authentic relationship through mutual self-awareness.

Cultivating self-awareness is an ongoing investment that enriches every aspect of life. It enables you to embrace your strengths, acknowledge your vulnerabilities, and act more intentionally in alignment with your values.

Through this journey, you will discover that self-acceptance is the foundation for personal growth and authentic relationships. Self-awareness also deepens your understanding of the world around you, as knowing yourself fosters greater empathy and connection with others.

Remember, self-awareness is not a destination but a continuous process of exploration and learning. Be kind to yourself and celebrate every step forward. By living with clarity and consciousness about who you are, you become better equipped to face challenges, seize opportunities, and create a life filled with purpose and meaning.

Law 43
Define Purpose

Defining a purpose is like lighting a guiding beacon amid life's uncertainties. It acts as a compass, helping you navigate daily choices and challenges with clarity, direction, and meaning. A purpose not only drives your actions but also fuels your motivation, resilience, and ability to overcome difficulties. It is an inner force connecting your values, passions, and talents, enabling you to live more authentically.

Purpose extends beyond temporary goals; it is rooted in your deepest beliefs, the legacy you wish to leave, and the way you want to impact the world. Living with purpose provides a sense of fulfillment and genuine happiness, as every effort gains meaning and each accomplishment becomes a step toward something greater.

This journey requires introspection, courage to face fears, and a commitment to transforming dreams into actions. Whether in everyday gestures or large-scale projects, your purpose reflects who you are and the impact you aspire to have on the world. By defining a clear purpose, you become not only the protagonist of your story but also an inspiration to others.

Personal Benefits

Direction and Clarity: A clear purpose provides guidance for your decisions and actions, helping you focus on meaningful goals and avoid wasting energy on distractions.

Motivation and Persistence: A significant purpose increases your determination to overcome obstacles and persist even in challenging situations.

Resilience and Recovery: A strong purpose acts as an anchor during crises, helping you bounce back from setbacks and find strength to move forward.

Happiness and Fulfillment: Living purposefully brings a deep sense of joy and satisfaction, as your efforts contribute to something greater than yourself.

Self-Discovery and Confidence: Pursuing a purpose fosters self-awareness and confidence, enabling you to understand your values, passions, and talents, and live authentically.

Positive Impact: Living with purpose allows you to make a difference in the world, contributing to meaningful causes and leaving a lasting legacy.

Methods of Application

Connect with Your Values:

Identify Core Values: Reflect on the principles that guide your actions and give you a sense of purpose and meaning.

Live by Your Values: Align your actions and decisions with these fundamental values to ensure authenticity in your life.

Prioritize What Matters: Focus your energy and time on activities and relationships that resonate with your core values.

Discover Your Passions:

Explore Your Interests: Dedicate time to exploring hobbies and activities that spark curiosity and bring you joy.

Recognize Your Talents: Identify your natural abilities and develop them in ways that bring satisfaction and achievement.

Notice Energizing Activities: Pay attention to what excites and motivates you, as these are often clues to your passions.

Turn Dreams Into Reality:

Set Goals: Break your dreams into clear, specific, and measurable goals, creating actionable plans to achieve them.

Overcome Fear and Insecurity: Face your fears with courage and take the first step toward realizing your dreams.

Seek Support and Inspiration: Surround yourself with supportive people and seek mentorship or resources to guide your journey.

Live Intentionally:

Make Conscious Choices: Spend your time, energy, and resources on activities aligned with your purpose.

Take Responsibility: Acknowledge that you are the creator of your life story and have the power to shape it.

Seek Balance: Harmonize different aspects of your life—personal, professional, social, and spiritual—for a fulfilling existence.

Step-by-Step Guide to Defining Purpose:

Connect with Your Values: Identify your core values, align your actions with them, and prioritize what matters most.

Discover Your Passions: Explore interests, recognize your talents, and focus on activities that energize you.

Turn Dreams into Reality: Set actionable goals, face fears, and seek support.

Live Intentionally: Make conscious choices, take responsibility, and balance your life.

Adjustments if Desired Results Are Not Achieved:

Struggling to Define Purpose: Engage in self-discovery exercises, consult with mentors, or explore guidance from a coach.

Feeling Lost or Demotivated: Revisit your passions, redefine your goals, and seek new sources of inspiration.

Difficulty Realizing Dreams: Break down objectives into manageable steps, create a detailed action plan, and celebrate small wins.

Examples:

Volunteer Work: A person discovers their purpose in helping others and commits to working with a nonprofit organization.

Creative Expression: An artist defines their purpose through art, sharing their perspective and inspiring audiences.

Social Entrepreneurship: An entrepreneur finds purpose in building a business that creates positive societal impact.

Defining and living with purpose is a transformative act. It provides a guiding light amidst life's uncertainties, strengthens your ability to overcome challenges, and deepens the joy of your achievements.

With a clear purpose, you not only achieve personal satisfaction but also contribute to the world in meaningful ways. Your choices and actions reflect your values and passions, infusing your life with coherence and authenticity.

Remember, discovering purpose is a continuous journey. It evolves with your growth and learning but remains rooted in the essence of who you are. By aligning your life with your purpose, you build a path of personal fulfillment and leave a legacy that positively influences others and transcends time.

Law 44
Seek Mentorship

No one achieves great goals alone. Seeking mentorship is a strategic step that accelerates personal and professional development, shortening the path to success. A mentor is more than a guide; they are a catalyst for learning, growth, and achievement. By sharing their experiences, knowledge, and worldview, a mentor offers not only guidance but also a support network that helps overcome challenges and identify opportunities that might otherwise go unnoticed.

Mentorship is not just about absorbing advice; it is a dynamic exchange process where the mentee learns to open up to feedback, reflect on their own values, and improve their skills. This relationship can transform doubts into clarity and challenges into stepping stones for progress. Finding a compatible mentor requires introspection, as you need to understand your goals and areas for development to know whom to seek.

With the support of a mentor, you expand your perspectives, strengthen your self-confidence, and develop essential skills to achieve your goals. It is a journey of learning, growth, and connection that, if well-nurtured, can positively impact not only your trajectory but also that of everyone around you.

Personal Advantages:

Accelerated Development: Mentorship provides guidance, advice, and personalized support, accelerating your personal and professional growth and shortening the learning curve.

Expanded Perspectives: A mentor shares their experiences, knowledge, and worldview, broadening your perspectives and offering new ways of thinking and acting.

Skill Development: A mentor helps identify your strengths and weaknesses and develop essential skills and competencies for success in your field.

Overcoming Challenges: A mentor provides support and guidance to overcome challenges and obstacles, sharing their own experiences and offering practical and strategic advice.

Increased Self-Confidence: A mentor's support and encouragement strengthen your self-confidence and belief in your ability to achieve your goals.

Building a Network: A mentor can introduce you to influential people in your field, expanding your network and opening doors to new opportunities.

Application Methods:

Identify Your Goals and Needs:

Define your mentorship goals: What do you hope to achieve through mentorship? What skills do you want to develop? What challenges do you need to overcome?

Identify your development areas: In which areas do you need more guidance and support? What weaknesses would you like to improve?

Determine the type of mentor you need: What kind of experience, knowledge, and profile would be most valuable for you at this point in your career?

Find a Compatible Mentor:

Search within your network: Talk to people you admire and respect who have relevant experience and knowledge in your area of interest.

Join mentorship programs: Look for mentorship programs in your company, university, or community that connect mentors and mentees based on their interests and goals.

Use online platforms: Explore online platforms that connect mentors and mentees in various fields.

Build a Trusting Relationship:

Communicate openly and transparently: Share your goals, expectations, and challenges with your mentor, and be open to listening to their advice and feedback.

Show respect and gratitude: Value your mentor's time and expertise, demonstrating appreciation for their availability and contribution to your development.

Be proactive and responsible: Take responsibility for your development, prepare for mentoring sessions, follow your mentor's advice, and strive to apply what you learn.

Make the Most of Mentorship:

Ask questions and seek clarity: Don't hesitate to ask questions and request clarifications to ensure you understand your mentor's advice and guidance.

Be open to feedback and constructive criticism: Be receptive to your mentor's feedback, even if it's hard to hear, and use constructive criticism as an opportunity for growth.

Share your progress and challenges: Keep your mentor updated on your progress, challenges, and doubts so they can offer appropriate support and guidance.

Cultivate the Relationship Long-Term:

Stay in regular contact: Maintain regular communication with your mentor, even after the formal mentorship program ends.

Show gratitude and recognition: Continue to express appreciation and recognition for your mentor's support and guidance throughout your career.

Pay it forward: When you gain more experience, consider becoming a mentor to others, sharing your knowledge and contributing to the development of new talents.

Step-by-Step Guide to Applying the "Seek Mentorship" Law:

Identify your goals and needs: Define what you aim to achieve through mentorship.

Find a compatible mentor: Search your network, join mentorship programs, or use online platforms.

Build a trusting relationship: Communicate openly, show respect, and be proactive.

Make the most of mentorship: Ask questions, stay open to feedback, and share your progress.

Cultivate the relationship long-term: Maintain contact, show gratitude, and pay it forward.

Adjustments if Expected Results Are Not Achieved:

Difficulty finding a mentor: Review your search criteria, expand your network, and consider different mentorship program options.

Unproductive mentorship relationship: Clearly communicate your expectations and needs, and if the relationship does not improve, consider finding a new mentor.

Failure to apply mentorship learnings: Create an action plan to implement your mentor's advice and regularly track your progress.

Examples:

A young professional seeking mentorship from an experienced executive to guide their career.

An entrepreneur seeking mentorship from an investor for advice on expanding their business.

An artist seeking mentorship from a more experienced artist to develop their skills and gain recognition in their field.

Seeking mentorship is an act of courage and humility, demonstrating your willingness to learn from others' experiences and grow intentionally and rapidly. A mentor offers more than practical advice; they provide inspiration, support, and the confidence needed to face challenges and turn goals into achievements.

Remember, mentorship is a two-way street. To maximize its benefits, be open to learning, apply the lessons in practice, and recognize the value of the time and knowledge your mentor dedicates to you. Cultivating this relationship can open doors, strengthen skills, and even inspire you to give back by becoming a mentor yourself in the future.

By investing in mentorship, you not only improve your chances of success but also build a legacy of learning and collaboration that transcends generations.

Law 45
Share Knowledge

Knowledge is one of the most valuable resources a person can possess, but its true power lies in its ability to be shared. When we share what we know, we not only help others grow but also deepen our own understanding. The "Share Knowledge" law invites us to let go of the idea that knowledge must be hoarded and instead promote the exchange of ideas as a driver for individual and collective progress.

By sharing knowledge, you expand your influence, build meaningful connections, and establish yourself as a reference in your field. This act is not limited to professional benefits; it also fosters a sense of purpose and contributes to societal evolution. The practice of sharing requires clarity, empathy, and the ability to communicate accessibly while encouraging dialogue and recognizing others' contributions.

Whether in a casual conversation, a speech before hundreds, or an article published online, the exchange of knowledge creates a virtuous cycle: teaching enriches the learner and strengthens the teacher. Thus, sharing is not just an act of generosity but also a powerful tool for growth and transformation.

Personal Advantages:

Deeper Understanding: Sharing what we know challenges us to organize our ideas, clarify doubts, and deepen our comprehension, contributing to more solid and lasting learning.

Building Relationships: Sharing knowledge creates opportunities to connect with others, promoting dialogue, the exchange of experiences, and the development of stronger personal and professional relationships.

Increased Visibility and Recognition: Sharing your knowledge on public platforms like blogs, social media, and events enhances your visibility and recognition as an expert in your field.

Communication Skill Development: Sharing knowledge helps develop written and verbal communication skills, enabling you to express your ideas clearly, concisely, and engagingly.

Professional Growth: Sharing knowledge and experiences with colleagues and professionals contributes to career growth, opening doors to new opportunities and collaborations.

Positive Societal Impact: By sharing your knowledge, you inspire and empower others to learn, grow, and achieve their goals, contributing to societal development.

Application Methods:

Identify Opportunities for Sharing:

Target Audience: Define who your audience is and what type of knowledge would be most relevant and useful to them.

Format: Choose the most suitable format for sharing your knowledge, such as articles, social media posts, lectures, workshops, mentoring, or online courses.

Channels: Identify the most effective channels to reach your audience, like blogs, websites, social media, live events, or online learning platforms.

Prepare Your Content with Clarity and Objectivity:

Organize Your Ideas: Structure your content logically and cohesively, using clear, objective, and accessible language for your target audience.

Use Visual Aids: Include images, graphs, videos, and other visuals to make your content more engaging and easier to understand.

Provide Examples and Context: Use practical examples, case studies, and real-life scenarios to illustrate your points and make the knowledge more relevant and applicable.

Build an Engaged Audience:

Share Relevant, High-Quality Content: Offer original, informative, and valuable content to your audience, establishing yourself as a reliable source of knowledge.

Engage with Your Audience: Respond to questions, comments, and messages to create dialogue and foster a connection with your audience.

Promote Your Content: Share your content across various channels and platforms, using digital marketing strategies to reach a broader audience.

Create a Collaborative Learning Environment:

Encourage Dialogue and Idea Exchange: Create spaces for discussions, debates, and the sharing of experiences, fostering a collaborative and enriching learning environment.

Be Open to Learning from Others: Recognize that knowledge is built collectively and remain open to learning from others' experiences and perspectives.

Share Credit and Acknowledge Contributions: When using others' knowledge, give due credit and recognize their contributions, promoting ethics and collaboration.

Step-by-Step Guide to Applying the "Share Knowledge" Law:

Identify opportunities: Define your audience, format, and sharing channels.

Prepare your content: Organize your ideas, use visual aids, and provide examples.

Build an audience: Share relevant content, interact with your audience, and promote your work.

Create a collaborative environment: Encourage dialogue, stay open to learning, and share credit.

Adjustments if Expected Results Are Not Achieved:

Difficulty Reaching Your Audience: Review your communication strategy, experiment with different channels and content formats, and actively promote your work.

Low Engagement with Your Content: Assess the quality and relevance of your content, seek audience feedback, and adjust your approach to meet their needs and interests.

Insecurity About Sharing Knowledge: Remember that everyone has something to share and that knowledge multiplies when shared. Start small, sharing with trusted individuals or groups, and gradually expand your reach.

Examples:

A teacher creating a blog to share insights about education and inspire other educators.

A programmer sharing video tutorials on coding to help others learn new skills and enter the job market.

A company hosting workshops and lectures to share experiences and best practices with others in the industry.

Sharing knowledge is more than transmitting information; it's about building bridges between people, ideas, and opportunities. This practice strengthens relationships, inspires change, and lays the foundation for a more collaborative and innovative community. When you share what you know, you allow others to shine while keeping the flame of learning alive within yourself.

Remember that each act of intellectual generosity can resonate far beyond the moment it occurs. Whether answering a question, mentoring someone, or contributing content for a wider audience, you leave a lasting impact.

So, adopt the habit of sharing. Transform your experiences into sources of inspiration, your lessons into guides for others, and your knowledge into a legacy that multiplies opportunities and creates a better future. By doing so, you not only help change the world around you but also reinforce your own journey of growth and fulfillment.

Law 46
Practice Gratitude

Gratitude is one of the most transformative and powerful emotions we can cultivate in our lives. It not only connects us to the positives in our daily experiences but also promotes well-being, strengthens relationships, and helps us find meaning in our experiences. By practicing gratitude, we recognize the value of both small and large blessings, turning challenges into lessons and difficulties into opportunities for growth.

The "Practice Gratitude" law invites us to view the world through a more optimistic and generous lens, encouraging us to appreciate what we have and what we share with others. This habit, though simple, has a profound impact on our mental, physical, and emotional health, while also creating a more welcoming and harmonious environment in our relationships.

Adopting gratitude as a lifestyle doesn't mean ignoring problems or denying adversity but rather developing the ability to find reasons to be thankful even amidst difficulties. Through a kind gesture, a moment of reflection, or a word of appreciation, gratitude becomes a practice that enriches both the giver and the receiver.

Personal Advantages:

Increased Happiness and Well-Being: Gratitude promotes the release of hormones like dopamine and serotonin, which generate feelings of pleasure, happiness, and emotional well-being.

Reduced Stress and Anxiety: Studies show that practicing gratitude lowers cortisol levels, the stress hormone, contributing to a calmer and more balanced mind.

Improved Physical Health: Gratitude strengthens the immune system, enhances sleep quality, and helps prevent cardiovascular diseases.

Stronger Relationships: Expressing gratitude for the people in your life strengthens emotional bonds, increases connection, and fosters healthier, more lasting relationships.

Enhanced Resilience: Gratitude helps develop resilience, enabling you to face challenges with greater optimism and find strength to overcome adversity.

Improved Performance and Productivity: Grateful people tend to be more motivated, engaged, and productive, achieving better results in various areas of life.

Application Methods:

Cultivate Gratitude in Daily Life:

Gratitude Journal: Keep a gratitude journal, writing down daily the things you feel thankful for, no matter how small they may seem.

Express Gratitude Verbally: Thank the people around you for their actions, support, and presence in your life.

Gratitude Letters: Write letters to people who have made a difference in your life, expressing your appreciation and recognition.

Moments of Reflection: Take time each day to reflect on the blessings and good things in your life.

Practice Gratitude in Relationships:

Appreciate Loved Ones: Show your appreciation and gratitude for the people you love by expressing your feelings and valuing their presence.

Forgive and Thank: Practice forgiveness and gratitude, even in difficult situations, recognizing the lessons learned and the positive aspects of each experience.

Cultivate Generosity: Share your time, resources, and love with others, practicing generosity and reciprocity in your relationships.

Expand Your Focus to Abundance:

Value the Little Things: Learn to appreciate small joys, such as a sunny day, a kind gesture, or a good conversation.

Focus on What You Have: Instead of dwelling on what you lack, concentrate on what you already have and be thankful for it.

Cultivate an Abundance Mindset: Believe that the universe is abundant and there is enough for everyone. Open yourself to receiving life's blessings and opportunities.

Turn Gratitude into a Habit:

Incorporate Gratitude into Your Routine: Develop daily gratitude habits, such as giving thanks before meals, writing in a gratitude journal, or practicing gratitude meditation.

Share Your Gratitude: Inspire others by sharing your gratitude, encouraging them to cultivate this feeling in their own lives.

Remember Gratitude in Difficult Times: In moments of challenge and adversity, recall the things you are grateful for to find strength and hope.

Step-by-Step Guide to Applying the "Practice Gratitude" Law:

Cultivate gratitude in daily life: Keep a gratitude journal, express verbal gratitude, and reflect regularly.

Practice gratitude in relationships: Appreciate loved ones, forgive, and cultivate generosity.

Expand your focus to abundance: Value the small things, focus on what you have, and nurture an abundance mindset.

Make gratitude a habit: Incorporate gratitude into your routine, share it with others, and remember it in tough times.

Adjustments if Expected Results Are Not Achieved:

Difficulty Feeling Gratitude: Start small, focusing on a few things you're grateful for, and gradually expand your focus to other areas of your life.

Feeling Unmotivated or Cynical: Remind yourself of gratitude's benefits for mental and physical health, and seek inspiration from stories of people who transformed their lives through gratitude.

Struggling to Maintain a Gratitude Habit: Create visual reminders, set a specific time for gratitude practice, and find creative ways to integrate gratitude into your routine.

Examples:

A person writing nightly in their gratitude journal, listing the good things that happened during the day.

A couple expressing gratitude to each other for their love, companionship, and support.

A work team celebrating the success of a project by acknowledging each member's contributions.

Practicing gratitude is a daily choice that transforms how we live and interact with the world. It connects us to often-overlooked positives, strengthens us in the face of challenges, and draws us closer to those who make our journey meaningful.

By cultivating gratitude, we create a virtuous cycle of positivity and reciprocity, inspiring others to do the same. Gratitude doesn't have to be grandiose; small gestures, like saying "thank you" or reflecting on joyful moments, can already make an impact.

Make gratitude a habit. Recognize and appreciate your achievements, celebrate your blessings, and express your gratitude to those around you. In doing so, you will not only enrich your life but also create a legacy of kindness, connection, and joy that continues to inspire and transform.

Law 47
Promote Well-Being

In a world that grows increasingly fast-paced and demanding, promoting well-being has become essential for living a balanced and meaningful life. This practice goes beyond physical health care, encompassing mental, emotional, and spiritual health, as well as fostering positive relationships and environments.

The "Promote Well-Being" law invites us to take a holistic approach to self-care. It emphasizes the importance of building healthy habits, such as balanced nutrition, regular physical activity, and stress management. It also encourages seeking balance between work and leisure, connecting with nature, and cultivating positive relationships.

Well-being is not merely a state to be achieved but a continuous process that requires attention and effort. Every small choice we make—from the people we surround ourselves with to the activities we incorporate into our routine—contributes to building a healthier, happier, and more harmonious life.

Personal Advantages:

Physical and Mental Health: Promoting well-being strengthens the immune system, prevents diseases, improves sleep quality, reduces stress and anxiety, and enhances mental health and emotional balance.

Increased Energy and Vitality: Caring for the body and mind boosts energy levels and vitality, allowing you to face daily challenges with greater enthusiasm and drive.

Improved Concentration and Productivity: Well-being enhances mental clarity, focus, and concentration, increasing productivity and efficiency in various areas of life.

Creativity and Innovation: A healthy mind and body stimulate creativity, imagination, and the ability to find innovative solutions to challenges.

Healthier Relationships: Well-being contributes to healthier, more positive relationships, increasing empathy, compassion, and the ability to connect with others.

Higher Self-Esteem and Confidence: Taking care of yourself and feeling good about yourself strengthens self-esteem, self-confidence, and self-image.

Application Methods:

Cultivate Healthy Habits:

Balanced Nutrition: Adopt a diet rich in fruits, vegetables, whole grains, and legumes while limiting processed foods, sugar, and saturated fats.

Regular Physical Activity: Engage in regular exercise, choosing intensity and types that suit your physical condition and preferences.

Restorative Sleep: Prioritize quality sleep by establishing a relaxing bedtime routine and creating an optimal sleep environment.

Stress Management: Practice stress management techniques such as meditation, yoga, deep breathing, and mindfulness to calm the mind and reduce anxiety.

Nurture the Mind and Body:

Foster Positive Thoughts: Practice optimism, gratitude, and positive thinking, focusing on the good in life and cultivating a growth mindset.

Connect with Nature: Spend time outdoors and enjoy the benefits of natural environments for mental and physical health.

Express Emotions: Find healthy ways to express your emotions, such as talking to friends, journaling, or engaging in artistic activities.

Prioritize Mental Health: Seek professional help if you face mental health challenges such as depression, anxiety, or post-traumatic stress.

Seek Balance:

Work-Life Balance: Set clear boundaries between work and personal life, and reserve time for hobbies, relationships, and enjoyable activities.

Leisure and Relaxation: Incorporate leisure and relaxation activities into your routine, such as reading, listening to music, watching movies, or spending time outdoors.

Social Connection: Foster positive relationships with friends, family, and loved ones, and participate in social activities that bring joy and connection.

Create a Well-Being Environment:

Organize Your Space: Create a clean, organized, and welcoming living and work environment that fosters inner peace and well-being.

Surround Yourself with Positive People: Build relationships with optimistic, inspiring individuals who bring joy and lightness to your life.

Practice Gratitude: Develop a habit of gratitude by acknowledging and appreciating life's blessings, no matter how small.

Step-by-Step Guide to Applying the "Promote Well-Being" Law:

Cultivate healthy habits: Balanced diet, physical exercise, restorative sleep, and stress management.

Nurture the mind and body: Positive thinking, connecting with nature, emotional expression, and mental health care.

Seek balance: Work-life harmony, leisure time, and social connections.

Create a well-being environment: Organized spaces, positive relationships, and gratitude practices.

Adjustments if Expected Results Are Not Achieved:

Difficulty Implementing Healthy Habits: Start with small changes in your routine, set realistic goals, and seek support from a health professional or coach.

Feeling Overwhelmed or Stressed: Identify factors contributing to stress and anxiety, and implement strategies to manage your emotions and prioritize activities.

Neglecting Well-Being: Remember that well-being is the foundation for a fulfilling and healthy life. Make it a priority and consciously choose activities that support this goal.

Examples:

A person practicing yoga and meditation regularly to relieve stress and foster emotional balance.

A professional dedicating time to exercise and maintain a healthy diet to boost energy and productivity at work.

A family gathering for a healthy dinner and pleasant conversation to strengthen bonds and promote collective well-being.

Promoting well-being is a powerful way to invest in yourself and create a solid foundation for all areas of life. By caring for your body, mind, and emotions, you gain energy, resilience, and clarity to face challenges and fully enjoy life's joys.

Remember that well-being is a personal journey. There's no need to transform everything at once; start with small changes, such as setting aside time for self-care or appreciating the positives around you. Over time, these practices will naturally become part of your routine.

By prioritizing well-being, you not only enrich your own life but also inspire and empower those around you, creating an atmosphere of health, happiness, and positivity. Embrace this law as a commitment to yourself and experience the benefits of a full, balanced life.

Law 48
Build Balance

Living with balance is essential for achieving a fulfilling and meaningful life. However, the modern world, with its increasing demands and high expectations, often pushes us toward imbalances that compromise our health, productivity, and emotional well-being. The "Build Balance" law guides us to harmonize the various aspects of our lives—personal, professional, social, and spiritual—reducing stress, increasing energy, and strengthening our relationships.

Balance is not a fixed goal but an ongoing practice that requires reflection, planning, and flexibility. It begins with recognizing our values and priorities, involves efficient management of time and energy, and culminates in adopting habits that promote integral health and well-being. By building balance, we not only enhance our quality of life but also become more resilient, creative, and fulfilled.

Personal Advantages:

Reduced Stress and Anxiety: Balance fosters inner harmony and reduces stress and anxiety caused by excessive demands in one or more areas of life.

Increased Productivity and Focus: Balancing different aspects of life allows you to focus better on each one, enhancing productivity and efficiency.

Improved Physical and Mental Health: Balance contributes to better physical and mental health, reducing the risk of stress-related illnesses like heart problems, depression, and anxiety.

Healthier Relationships: Balance enables you to dedicate time and energy to your relationships, strengthening bonds and creating meaningful connections.

Greater Creativity and Fulfillment: Balance creates space for creativity, inspiration, and the pursuit of new experiences, making life more rewarding and joyful.

Enhanced Self-Esteem and Self-Awareness: By understanding yourself better and identifying your priorities, you can create a life aligned with your values, boosting self-esteem and self-awareness.

Methods of Application:

Define Your Priorities:

Identify Values and Goals: Reflect on your short- and long-term values and goals to gain clarity on what truly matters to you.

Prioritize Life Areas: Analyze the various areas of your life—personal, professional, social, spiritual—and define your priorities in each.

Set Realistic Goals: Establish achievable goals in each area to avoid overloading yourself or succumbing to perfectionism.

Manage Your Time and Energy:

Organize Your Time: Use tools like calendars, spreadsheets, or apps to plan activities, set deadlines, and prioritize tasks.

Learn to Say "No": Don't hesitate to decline commitments that don't align with your priorities or that drain your energy unproductively.

Delegate Tasks: Whenever possible, delegate tasks to others to free up time and energy for more important and strategic activities.

Cultivate Flexibility:

Adapt to Change: Be open to changes and unexpected events, and adjust your plans and priorities as needed.

Balance Discipline and Spontaneity: Find a middle ground between planning and spontaneity, allowing room for creativity and the unexpected.

Learn from Mistakes: Don't dwell on occasional imbalances; view mistakes as learning opportunities and adjust your strategies for better balance in the future.

Practice Habits That Promote Balance:

Physical Exercise and Healthy Eating: Maintain a routine of physical activity and balanced nutrition to promote physical and mental health.

Relaxation and Self-Connection: Set aside time for relaxing activities, like meditation, yoga, reading, or quiet reflection.

Healthy Relationships: Invest time and energy in nurturing supportive relationships with family, friends, and loved ones.

Pursuit of Purpose and Meaning: Engage in activities that bring you satisfaction and meaning, aligning your actions with your values and passions.

Step-by-Step Guide to Applying the "Build Balance" Law:

Define Priorities: Identify your values, goals, and priorities in every area of life.

Manage Time and Energy: Plan your time, say "no" when necessary, and delegate tasks.

Cultivate Flexibility: Adapt to changes, balance discipline and spontaneity, and learn from mistakes.

Practice Balance-Promoting Habits: Exercise regularly, eat healthily, relax, nurture relationships, and seek purpose.

Adjustments if Expected Results Are Not Achieved:

Feeling Overwhelmed in One Area of Life: Reassess your priorities, redistribute your time and energy, and simplify your commitments.

Neglecting a Life Area: Identify the source of imbalance and find ways to dedicate more time and attention to that area by redefining priorities and creating new habits.

Feeling Unmotivated or Drained: Engage in activities that bring you joy, reignite your passions, and reconnect with your life purpose to regain enthusiasm and vitality.

Examples:

A professional setting clear boundaries between work and personal life, reserving time for family, hobbies, and physical activities.

A student balancing studies with extracurricular activities, leisure time, and friendships.

An individual seeking balance among body, mind, and spirit by practicing meditation, yoga, and maintaining a healthy diet.

Building balance is a commitment to yourself—a conscious choice to prioritize what truly matters and let go of what doesn't add value to your life. Though challenging, this practice yields invaluable rewards: greater clarity, focus, energy, and happiness.

Remember, balance is dynamic—it evolves with circumstances and life stages. Cultivate flexibility and remain attentive to areas that need more focus. Small, regular adjustments can profoundly impact your well-being and harmony between your goals and values.

By embracing the "Build Balance" law, you not only care for yourself but also inspire others to pursue a more aligned and meaningful life. Let your choices reflect what's most important, and let balance be the foundation of your achievements and happiness.

Law 49
Create Impact

Creating impact is the essence of living a life that transcends the individual and contributes to something greater. The "Create Impact" law teaches that it's not just about making a difference, but about doing so consciously, intentionally, and in alignment with your values and skills. In a world filled with challenges and opportunities, every positive action generates a ripple effect, inspiring others to do the same and creating a cycle of transformation.

By engaging in causes that resonate with your ideals, you expand your purpose, build meaningful relationships, and create a legacy that will echo beyond the present. No matter the scale of your action—from local initiatives to global projects—what truly matters is the intentionality and commitment to fostering change for the common good.

Personal Advantages:

Purpose and Meaning: Creating impact brings purpose and meaning to your life, connecting you with something larger than yourself and encouraging intentional living.

Personal and Professional Fulfillment: Contributing to the common good and making a difference in the world provides a deep sense of personal and professional achievement.

Increased Self-Esteem and Confidence: Making a positive impact boosts self-esteem and confidence by helping you recognize your potential to transform the world around you.

Strengthened Relationships: Engaging in purposeful causes and projects connects you with like-minded individuals, fostering stronger and more meaningful relationships.

Skill and Competency Development: Creating impact requires developing skills such as leadership, communication, creativity, and problem-solving, fostering personal and professional growth.

A Lasting Legacy: Your actions and contributions to the world leave a legacy that inspires and impacts people for generations.

Methods of Application:

Identify Relevant Causes:

Connect with Your Values: Reflect on your values and beliefs to identify causes that are important to you and motivate you to take action.

Analyze the World's Needs: Observe the challenges and problems affecting your community and the world to identify areas where you can make a difference.

Seek Inspiration from Others: Learn from people who are making a positive impact in the world, drawing inspiration from their stories and actions.

Develop Purposeful Projects:

Set Clear Goals: Define measurable goals for your projects, specifying the impact you aim to achieve and how you'll measure success.

Create an Action Plan: Develop a detailed plan outlining the steps, resources, and timelines required to implement your project.

Build Partnerships and Collaborations: Join forces with individuals and organizations that share your goals to amplify your impact and achieve meaningful results.

Mobilize People:

Share Your Vision: Clearly and inspiringly communicate your vision and objectives, motivating others to join your cause.

Lead by Example: Be a model of action and commitment, inspiring others to follow your lead.

Foster Collaboration: Create an environment of collaboration where everyone feels valued and motivated to contribute their skills and ideas.

Communicate Your Impact:

Share Success Stories: Highlight impactful stories from your work to show how your actions are making a difference in the world.

Use Metrics and Data: Present quantitative and qualitative data to demonstrate the impact of your efforts.

Inspire Others to Act: Share your experiences and lessons learned to encourage others to engage in social causes and create their own positive impact.

Step-by-Step Guide to Applying the "Create Impact" Law:

Identify Relevant Causes: Reflect on your values, assess the world's needs, and seek inspiration.

Develop Purposeful Projects: Set clear goals, create an action plan, and seek partnerships.

Mobilize People: Share your vision, lead by example, and foster collaboration.

Communicate Your Impact: Share success stories, use metrics, and inspire others to act.

Adjustments if Expected Results Are Not Achieved:

Difficulty Identifying a Relevant Cause: Explore different fields, talk to people working in social causes, and try volunteering to discover your passions.

Project Not Achieving Desired Impact: Review your objectives, adjust your strategy, and seek feedback from those benefiting from your work.

Feeling Unmotivated or Discouraged: Reconnect with your purpose, reignite your passion, and celebrate small victories along the way.

Examples:

A doctor dedicating time to provide free medical care to underserved communities, positively impacting their health and quality of life.

A teacher launching a literacy program for adults, empowering individuals and creating new opportunities for their futures.

A young entrepreneur developing an app to connect volunteers with social organizations, facilitating community engagement and amplifying positive impact.

Creating impact is both a choice and a calling. It requires courage to act, resilience to overcome challenges, and generosity to share your achievements. The rewards of this effort are plentiful: personal fulfillment, strengthened communities, and a world marked by your positive contributions.

Remember, creating impact isn't about achieving perfection but about doing your best with the resources you have. Celebrate every step forward, inspire others to join your cause, and stay connected to the purpose that drives you. By doing so, your life will stand as proof that with dedication and compassion, each individual has the power to transform the world.

Law 50
Reinvent Yourself

The "Reinvent Yourself" law invites you to embrace transformation as an essential part of life's journey. In a constantly evolving world, reinvention is not just a response to external changes but also an opportunity for internal growth, self-discovery, and the realization of new dreams.

Reinvention means challenging the status quo, questioning ingrained beliefs, and breaking free from limiting patterns that restrict your potential. It's about exploring the unknown with courage, developing new skills, and opening yourself to possibilities that once seemed out of reach. With every step, you move closer to a life more aligned with your values, passions, and purpose, building a future where the only constant is continuous progress.

Personal Advantages:

Adaptability and Resilience: Reinventing yourself enhances your ability to adapt and remain resilient in the face of life's changes and challenges, enabling you to navigate new scenarios with confidence and ease.

Personal and Professional Growth: Reinvention drives personal and professional growth, unlocking new opportunities, challenges, and experiences that foster learning and evolution.

Increased Creativity and Innovation: By challenging yourself and exploring new possibilities, you stimulate creativity and innovation, discovering original solutions and thriving in a dynamic world.

Breaking Limiting Patterns: Reinvention allows you to identify and break free from behaviors and beliefs that limit your potential.

Self-Knowledge and Confidence: The process of reinvention fosters self-awareness and confidence, connecting you with your essence, values, and deepest aspirations.

Achievement of Dreams and Purpose: Reinvention clears the path to achieving dreams and purposes that once felt distant or impossible, empowering you to live a more authentic and aligned life.

Methods of Application:

Question Your Beliefs and Perspectives:

Challenge the Status Quo: Reassess your beliefs, values, and perspectives, and stay open to new ways of thinking and seeing the world.

Seek New Experiences: Try new activities, explore different cultures, and connect with people from diverse backgrounds to broaden your horizons.

Analyze Behavior Patterns: Identify and understand the origins and impacts of limiting behaviors and thought patterns in your life.

Break Free from Limiting Patterns:

Identify Limiting Beliefs: Recognize beliefs that hinder your growth, such as doubts about your abilities, potential, or worthiness.

Face Your Fears: Confront fears and insecurities, stepping outside your comfort zone to explore new possibilities and overcome limitations.

Adopt a Growth Mindset: Embrace the belief in your ability to learn, develop, and adapt to changes, fostering continuous personal growth.

Develop New Skills:

Invest in Education and Training: Enroll in courses, workshops, and training programs to acquire new skills and knowledge aligned with your goals.

Learn from Mistakes: View errors as opportunities for growth, embracing experimentation and resilience in the face of setbacks.

Seek Mentorship and Inspiration: Connect with individuals who inspire you and can share their experiences and insights, guiding your reinvention journey.

Embrace Change and Uncertainty:

Cultivate Flexibility: Be open to adjusting your plans and adapting to new circumstances with agility and optimism.

Trust Your Intuition: Rely on your instincts when making important decisions in your life.

Celebrate Achievements: Acknowledge and celebrate milestones, no matter how small, and use them as motivation to keep evolving.

Step-by-Step Guide to Applying the "Reinvent Yourself" Law:

Question Beliefs and Perspectives: Challenge the status quo, explore new experiences, and analyze limiting patterns.

Break Limiting Patterns: Identify restrictive beliefs, confront fears, and adopt a growth mindset.

Develop New Skills: Invest in education, learn from mistakes, and seek mentorship.

Embrace Change: Stay flexible, trust your intuition, and celebrate your progress.

Adjustments if Expected Results Are Not Achieved:

Difficulty Leaving Your Comfort Zone: Start with small changes in your routine, experiment with new activities, and seek support from encouraging individuals.

Resistance to Change: Identify the root causes of resistance, work on limiting beliefs, and focus on developing adaptability and flexibility.

Feeling Lost or Unmotivated: Revisit your dreams and goals, draw inspiration from stories of successful reinvention, and reconnect with your passion for life.

Examples:

A professional changing careers after years in the same field, pursuing new challenges and a role more aligned with their interests and values.

An artist exploring new forms of expression, reinventing their style, and discovering creative possibilities.

An entrepreneur adapting to market changes by reinventing their business model and finding innovative ways to generate value.

Reinventing yourself is an act of courage and resilience that requires flexibility, determination, and a clear vision of who you want to become. Every choice, lesson, and challenge faced during this process brings you closer to a more authentic and empowered version of yourself.

Remember, reinvention doesn't have to be a giant leap—small steps often lead to the greatest transformations. Celebrate every bit of progress, no matter how modest, and trust in your ability to adapt, learn, and grow. By reinventing yourself, you not only transform your life but also inspire those around you to do the same, creating a lasting impact on the world.

Law 51
Live with Purpose

Living with purpose means embracing the essence of what makes us unique, aligning our actions with the values and passions that give meaning to our existence. When we live with purpose, our choices become intentional rather than random, guiding us toward a more fulfilling life connected to something greater than ourselves.

This journey begins with deep reflection on what truly matters to you. Your decisions become informed by your most genuine convictions, and each step you take reflects a commitment to what you believe. Living with purpose not only transforms your own life but also positively impacts the world around you, building a legacy of inspiration and contribution.

Personal Advantages:

Clarity and Direction: Living with purpose provides clarity and direction, helping you make conscious choices aligned with your values and goals.

Motivation and Persistence: A strong sense of purpose boosts your motivation and persistence, enabling you to overcome obstacles and pursue your dreams, even in the face of challenges.

Resilience and Growth: Purpose strengthens your resilience and ability to find strength and meaning during difficult times.

Happiness and Well-Being: Studies show that people who live with purpose are generally happier, experience greater psychological well-being, and lead more satisfying lives.

Connection and Belonging: Purpose fosters a connection to something greater—whether a cause, a community, or a transcendental value—providing a sense of belonging and meaning.

Positive Impact: Living with purpose allows you to make a meaningful difference in the world, contributing to the common good and leaving a legacy for future generations.

Methods of Application:

Integrate Your Values and Passions into Your Choices:

Identify Core Values: Reflect on your deepest values—those that guide your actions and represent your true essence.

Connect with Your Passions: Explore your interests and identify activities that bring you joy, satisfaction, and a sense of fulfillment.

Align Choices with Values and Passions: Make conscious decisions about how to spend your time, energy, and resources, prioritizing activities and relationships that resonate with your values and passions.

Cultivate Meaningful Relationships:

Build Authentic Connections: Invest in relationships rooted in trust, mutual respect, and shared values and purposes.

Support Others' Growth: Encourage and support the development of those around you by sharing your knowledge, experiences, and care.

Surround Yourself with Inspiration: Create a network of positive, motivated people who share your values and worldview.

Contribute to the Greater Good:

Find Your Cause: Identify a cause or purpose beyond yourself that inspires you to take action and make a difference.

Engage in Positive Actions: Participate in social projects, nonprofit organizations, or initiatives that promote the well-being of your community and the planet.

Use Your Talents for Good: Leverage your skills, abilities, and resources to contribute to building a better world.

Build a Legacy Reflecting Your Essence:

Live Intentionally: Make conscious choices that reflect your values, passions, and purposes, leaving a positive legacy for future generations.

Share Your Story: Inspire and motivate others by sharing your experiences, lessons, and journey.

Create Something Lasting: Develop something that transcends your existence, such as art, a socially impactful business, or a project that benefits your community.

Step-by-Step Guide to Applying the "Live with Purpose" Law:

Integrate Your Values and Passions: Identify your values, connect with your passions, and align your choices with them.

Cultivate Meaningful Relationships: Build authentic connections, support others, and surround yourself with inspiration.

Contribute to the Greater Good: Find a cause, engage in positive actions, and use your talents for meaningful contributions.

Build a Legacy: Live intentionally, share your story, and create something lasting.

Adjustments if Expected Results Are Not Achieved:

Feeling Lost or Directionless: Revisit your values, explore your passions, and seek experiences that bring clarity and purpose.

Difficulty Finding Meaning in Actions: Connect with inspiring causes, seek volunteer opportunities, and contribute to your community's well-being.

Feeling Disconnected from Others: Invest in authentic relationships, communicate openly, and seek out people who share your values and vision.

Examples:

An activist dedicating their life to advocating for human rights, finding purpose in defending the vulnerable and building a more just society.

An artist expressing their creativity and worldview through their work, leaving a legacy of beauty and inspiration for future generations.

An entrepreneur creating a business with social impact, generating jobs, promoting community development, and contributing to a sustainable future.

Living with purpose transforms challenges into lessons, relationships into meaningful connections, and actions into positive impact. It's an act of courage and authenticity that empowers you to walk a path aligned with your essence, fostering personal fulfillment and leaving lasting marks on the world.

Each small gesture aligned with your purpose is a step toward a more meaningful and joyful life. No matter where you are in your journey, it's always possible to recalibrate your direction and embrace what truly matters. By living with purpose, you become an inspiration to others and an example of how extraordinary life can be when guided by what we value most.

Law 52
Transcend Limits

Life is filled with limits—some imposed by the world around us, others stemming from beliefs and fears we carry internally. To transcend these limits is to embrace freedom, expand your potential, and create an extraordinary life. This practice requires courage, self-confidence, and a willingness to challenge the status quo, break free from limiting patterns, and explore new possibilities.

When we commit to transcending our limits, we become agents of transformation—not only in our own lives but also in the lives of those around us. This journey involves confronting fears, questioning conventions, and cultivating a broader, more inclusive vision of the world. It connects us to our true potential and inspires us to innovate, create, and contribute to a more abundant and courageous world.

Personal Advantages:

Freedom and Autonomy: Transcending limits frees you from the constraints of a mediocre, restricted life, allowing you to live with greater freedom, autonomy, and authenticity.

Expansion of Potential: By overcoming your barriers and believing in your unlimited potential, you pave the way for growth, achieving dreams, and reaching extraordinary goals.

Overcoming Challenges: Transcending limits strengthens your resilience and persistence to overcome challenges, transforming obstacles into opportunities for growth.

Personal Growth and Self-Awareness: The quest to transcend limits drives self-discovery, self-confidence, and personal development, enabling you to connect with your essence and express your true potential.

Creativity and Innovation: Challenging the status quo and exploring new possibilities awakens creativity and innovation, leading to unique solutions and extraordinary achievements.

Inspiration to Others: By transcending your own limits, you inspire and motivate those around you to do the same, contributing to a more courageous, creative, and abundant world.

Methods of Application:

Challenge the Status Quo:

Question Rules and Conventions: Don't blindly accept societal rules and norms. Critically evaluate established standards and understand their rationale.

Seek Different Perspectives: Open yourself to diverse viewpoints, cultures, and ways of thinking to broaden your horizons.

Be a Change Agent: Propose new ideas and solutions without fear. Serve as a catalyst for positive changes in your community and beyond.

Break Free from Limiting Beliefs:

Identify Limiting Beliefs: Pay attention to thoughts and beliefs that restrict your growth, and question their validity.

Overcome Fear: Recognize and confront your fears with courage and confidence, freeing yourself from what holds you back.

Cultivate Self-Confidence: Believe in your abilities and unlimited potential. Self-confidence is the foundation for challenging your limits and achieving greatness.

Cultivate the Courage to Be Authentic:

Stay True to Yourself: Embrace who you are, including your qualities and imperfections. Celebrate your individuality and express your authenticity fearlessly.

Follow Your Intuition: Trust your inner voice and instincts when making important life decisions.

Stand by Your Values: Have the courage to uphold your values and beliefs, even when they challenge the norm or face opposition.

Expand Your Horizons:

Seek Knowledge: Develop a habit of continuous learning by exploring new subjects, acquiring new skills, and expanding your knowledge.

Travel and Experience New Cultures: Exposure to different cultures broadens your worldview and challenges your perspectives.

Connect with Diverse People: Build relationships with individuals from varied backgrounds to enrich your life with fresh perspectives and experiences.

Step-by-Step Guide to Applying the "Transcend Limits" Law:

Challenge the Status Quo: Question rules, seek diverse perspectives, and become a change agent.

Break Free from Limiting Beliefs: Identify limiting beliefs, confront fears, and cultivate self-confidence.

Cultivate Authenticity: Stay true to yourself, trust your intuition, and uphold your values.

Expand Your Horizons: Pursue knowledge, explore new cultures, and connect with diverse individuals.

Adjustments if Expected Results Are Not Achieved:

Feeling Stuck in Limiting Patterns: Identify the beliefs and fears holding you back, and work to overcome them through therapy, coaching, or mentoring.

Difficulty Leaving Your Comfort Zone: Start with small challenges, gradually expand your limits, and celebrate each achievement along the way.

Feeling Demotivated or Doubtful: Revisit your dreams and purpose, draw inspiration from those who have transcended their own limits, and reconnect with your passion for life.

Examples:

An athlete recovering from a severe injury and returning to compete at a high level, defying the limits of body and mind.

An artist breaking away from traditional conventions, creating a unique style that expresses their individuality authentically.

An entrepreneur investing in an innovative business, defying market trends and creating a product or service that transforms lives.

Transcending limits is a bold choice that turns barriers into stepping stones for personal and collective growth. By challenging what seems impossible and embracing authenticity, you uncover your true strength.

Each step on this journey not only expands your horizons but also inspires others to explore the boundless power within themselves. The freedom to live beyond limits is a privilege we can all achieve. It takes courage to take the first step and determination to keep moving forward. By transcending your own limits, you become the best version of yourself and leave a profound impact on the world.

Epilogue

As this journey comes to a close, it's essential to reflect on the steps taken and the lessons embraced. You are no longer the same person who began this reading. Each concept explored here—from mastering your emotions to the art of planning victories—was designed to inspire action, clarity, and transformation. This is not just the end of a book; it is the beginning of a new way of thinking and acting.

The strategies shared transcend any specific context. They are universal tools, applicable to both professional and personal spheres, whether in the pursuit of grand objectives or in resolving everyday conflicts. The science thoroughly discussed throughout these pages underpins each technique, offering the assurance that they not only work but also have the potential to create profound and lasting change.

At this point, it's impossible not to look back and see how much power you already possess. The self-awareness gained here serves as a compass, guiding you toward more assertive decisions and more meaningful relationships. You now understand that shaping intentions or mastering narratives isn't about manipulation but about creating balance and clarity in often challenging interactions.

This book was not merely meant to inform but to empower. It is a constant invitation to practice. The true mastery of any strategy lies not in knowing it but in implementing it, refining it, and adapting it to the ever-evolving contexts of your life. The learning here is not static; it is dynamic, alive, ready to transform as you transform.

Now, the most important question remains: how will you use this knowledge? The pages may have been completed, but their impact depends entirely on what you decide to do from this moment forward. The world is full of distractions and noise, but those who master the strategies presented here not only survive them—they thrive, influence, and inspire.

May this work be more than a guide; may it serve as a reminder that strategic power lies in your hands. The ability to shape your life and your outcomes depends, above all, on the courage to apply what you've learned. This is the moment to turn intention into action and knowledge into results.

The end of a book, like in life, is not the end of everything. It is merely the beginning of a new narrative—and the pen is now in your hands.

www.ingramcontent.com/pod-product-compliance
Lightning Source LLC
LaVergne TN
LVHW040050080526
838202LV00045B/3564